brilliant

questions for great interviewers

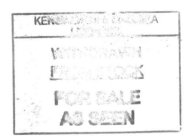

KENSINGTON & CHELSEA
LIBRARIES

WITHDRAWN
FROM STOCK

FOR SALE
AS SEEN

3 0116 01868281 3

questions for great interviewers

How to make sure you have the
right person for the job

Dee Walker

Prentice Hall
is an imprint of

Harlow, England • London • New York • Boston • San Francisco • Toronto • Sydney • Singapore • Hong Kong
Tokyo • Seoul • Taipei • New Delhi • Cape Town • Madrid • Mexico City • Amsterdam • Munich • Paris • Milan

PEARSON EDUCATION LIMITED

Edinburgh Gate
Harlow CM20 2JE
Tel: +44 (0)1279 623623
Fax: +44 (0)1279 431059
Website: www.pearsoned.co.uk

First published in Great Britain in 2010

© Pearson Education Limited 2010

The right of Dee Walker to be identified as author of this work has
been asserted by her in accordance with the Copyright, Designs and
Patents Act 1988.

ISBN: 978-0-273-73048-4

British Library Cataloguing-in-Publication Data
A catalogue record for this book is available from the British Library

Library of Congress Cataloging-in-Publication Data
A catalog record for this book is available from the Library of Congress

All rights reserved. No part of this publication may be reproduced, stored in a
retrieval system, or transmitted in any form or by any means, electronic,
mechanical, photocopying, recording or otherwise, without either the prior
written permission of the publisher or a licence permitting restricted copying in
the United Kingdom issued by the Copyright Licensing Agency Ltd, Saffron
House, 6–10 Kirby Street, London EC1N 8TS. This book may not be lent,
resold, hired out or otherwise disposed of by way of trade in any form of
binding or cover other than that in which it is published, without the prior
consent of the publisher.

10 9 8 7 6 5 4 3 2 1
14 13 12 11 10

Typeset in 10/14pt Plantin by 30
Printed and bound in Great Britain by Henry Ling Ltd., at the Dorset Press,
Dorchester, Dorset

The publisher's policy is to use paper manufactured from sustainable forests.

To Stephen Cranmer, for his unlimited patience while I was writing this book.

Contents

About the author

Dee Walker has been recruiting for over 30 years. Having worked in Human Resources she decided to specialise in the recruitment sector and has made hiring decisions for her employers, clients and her own business and, throughout her career, has successfully trained new interviewers.

For 15 years Dee was a Director of Hudson Walker International Ltd., which she set up with a business partner in the recession of the early nineties. The company works with both UK and international clients (www.hudsonwalker.com). She moved into commercial recruiting from Harrods where she had been Recruitment Manager.

She has interviewed at all levels from office juniors through to managing directors and across all categories from carpenters to chefs, marketeers to merchandisers, logistics to legal staff and everything in between.

Having worked with line managers, she understands the problems they can have when faced with interviewing – lack of training and experience in this area combined with a demanding schedule often puts recruiting at the bottom of their priorities. It was to help these managers and the growing number of owner drivers that she has written this book.

Acknowledgements

I would like to thank Pauline Hudson-Evans.

Introduction

Who should read this book, why and how to use it

Hiring the right person for the job is crucial in any business. After all, hiring the wrong candidate can be very expensive – you may have to pay them off, re-hire, spend time and money re-training and deal with disruption caused within the team.

This book is designed to assist anyone involved in the recruitment process who has little or no interview or selection experience or training, and it can be used for any type of role at any level.

It is divided into three easy reference stages:

- Part One covers the pre-interview planning.
- Part Two the interviews and the questions you need to ask.
- Part Three how to ensure you hire the right candidate and avoid discrimination.

For those who have total responsibility for the recruitment process it takes you through all the stages from defining the role through to the offer. Your usual method of selecting candidates may be with a straightforward interview, but there are other elements you could include. Telephone interviews will save time, and including a practical task will highlight more functional skills.

For others who are asked to conduct first or second interviews as part of the recruitment process it allows you to dip into the relevant chapters.

As you will be fitting recruitment in and around your everyday work schedule there will be tips on how to make the best use of your time, with easy-to-use summaries and plans for quick reference.

If you have been involved in recruiting before some of these questions will highlight the problems.

- Have you ever hired the wrong person for a role, and why was that?
- Did you then realise that this issue could and should have been picked up at interview?
- Ever felt under-prepared, and the interview has ended up as a 'chat'?
- Lost for words and not sure what to ask next?
- Felt that you don't have the information you need but not sure how to get it?
- Had to finish an interview without being able to assess the candidate?
- Thought that the interview could have gone better?
- Forgotten to give the candidate some vital information?
- How successful was that recruitment and could it have been better?

Alternatively this may be the first time you have been involved in or responsible for recruiting someone, so you will be considering the following:

- How are you going to start?
- How do you know what you are looking for?
- What exactly are the services recruitment consultants can offer?
- Can advertising agencies help you recruit?
- Where do you search for candidates?

- What are you going to ask at interview?
- What salary should you offer?

The book is written in jargon-free language so you do not have to be a personnel or human resource expert to understand it. If you are to become part of the recruitment process there are some terms you will come across regularly, such as 'job specification' for the document explaining what duties and responsibilities the job holder will have and 'candidate specification or profile' explaining what skills and experience you are looking for in the candidate. Where technical terms like these are used there is a definition to help you understand what is meant when others use this vocabulary.

Mistakes in recruitment are often made because of lack of preparation from the outset. The job content or the candidate requirements have not been thought through, resulting in someone being hired to do a job that is significantly different from what they expected. Early evaluation of these needs is essential but it does not have to be time-consuming.

Similarly, interviews should be focussed and concentrate on assessing the candidate against the skills needed for the job. They should not be 'chats' where you end up hiring the candidate you liked the best but not necessarily the most suited.

Inexperienced interviewers can end up finding themselves floundering for the next question to ask because they have been using the wrong type of questions, or can get to the end of an interview and still not know if the person is suitable. Here we will look at types of questions and how to use them, as well as specific questions for different situations. It will also help those who are not used to interviewing or not comfortable in that situation by giving clear ways of planning your interview and the questions you need to ask. You will then be able to take control of making sure you get all the information you need to make a valued decision on whom to hire.

You will gain the confidence to keep asking questions until you have ALL the information you need and will never be stuck for a question again.

The questions can be used for all levels of candidates but there are specific guides for school and college leavers as well as more senior candidates.

After all this hard work you really do need to make sure you have an offer the candidate is interested in, so in Part Three there are guidelines on how to structure and make your offer.

With more and more employment legislation it is becoming essential to make sure that not only do you hire the right person but you do so in a way that is fair to everyone. For those of you who do not have the benefit of in-house human resource experts, *Brilliant Questions for Great Interviewers* will help to de-mystify some of the legislation on discrimination and how you can avoid it.

By the end of the book you will be able to:

- Identify what the job involves.
- Identify what experience and skills the candidate must have and those that will be useful but not essential.
- Source candidates.
- Decide on what to include as part of the recruitment process.
- Shortlist for interview.
- Interview and get the information needed to make an informed decision.
- Understand the legal aspects to ensure you are not prejudiced in their selection.
- Save time and money in the process and by hiring the best candidate.
- Have a battery of 'brilliant' questions.

- Make the offer.
- Get the candidate started.

Staff are a major investment – ensure you get the right return.

PART 1

Before you interview

CHAPTER 1

Identifying the needs of the business

Compiling the job specification

When someone resigns it should be seen as an opportunity to redefine the job and the type of person you need in it. Usually it fills most managers with dread – another problem they have to deal with on top of everything else. Don't panic. You will have enough information readily to hand to make a start on the recruiting and you may even have an old job specification you can use as a starting point.

What to do first

Understanding what you are looking for will help you find it. Some time spent now in these early stages will save time and money in the long run

> understanding what you are looking for will help you find it

and will help you hire the best. Whether you are recruiting a new person into an existing role or for an entirely new role to the business, you need to identify what that role is.

 brilliant definition

The **job specification** or **job definition** is the document that outlines who the job reports to, the main function / overall objective of the role, details the specific duties and responsibilities that will be included in the job, and the remuneration package.

Recruiting a new candidate into an existing role

Even though this role already exists and you may have a job specification for it, spend a few moments reviewing it and ask yourself the following questions:

Ⓠ How has your business changed since you hired the person who has just resigned?

Ⓠ How has the role changed?

Ⓠ Have they changed it? Some employees adapt roles and end up spending the majority of their time on the parts they enjoy most and vice versa.

Ⓠ Perhaps you didn't hire the present incumbent and you have always felt that there could be someone more suitable for the job or with a different skill set. What other or different skills do you want now?

Ⓠ If the outgoing employee has done a good job, then get them involved in helping you select the next candidate and take the pressure off you. Can they suggest an area where they felt they struggled and advise that you need to look for different experience in someone new?

Ⓠ Do they actually need to be replaced?

Ⓠ Could some of their tasks be better assigned elsewhere?

Ⓠ Can you afford not to replace or hire this person? Saving money is always important no matter what the current economic situation, and the cost of hiring is expensive on top of the annual salary and employment costs. You also need to think about the bigger picture and the impact that not having someone in this role may make on the rest of the team, your customers, etc. One may outweigh the other.

Ⓠ How vital is this role within the overall business and within the team?

Ⓠ Does this role report to the correct line manager? As your business has changed and the role has developed, it may be better placed in another function.

 **example**

Consider the secretary hired as a vital part of the business working for two partners in recruitment several years ago. As technology improved, the partners found it easier to amend CVs on-screen rather than having her re-type them. There were no confirmation of interview letters needed as this was all done on email. The major part of the role had disappeared. The secretary concerned was still busy but now much more involved in office and facilities management. When she resigned it needed careful consideration regarding what the job now involved and what skills were needed to fill it. Office management was now the main function of the job and secretarial skills were not even needed.

So what is the job?

Somewhere on your system you may have the old job specification. However, it may be one that was written before you joined or just completely out-of-date. Take a look at it and decide if it is still valid but what changes are needed, if any. By preparing now and ensuring you know what the job is and what kind of person you need to fill it you will be able to more closely match candidates to your current requirements.

If you do not review and update the details, candidates will be selected on out-of-date information. They may meet the old criteria but you will realise during the interviews that your needs have changed and you need candidates with different skills. This will mean going back to the start, having wasted valuable time and costs.

If the job specification is no longer appropriate or you don't have one, then write one. It will help you focus on what you need, and you can then use it as the base for briefing recruiters, advertising and so on, and to match the candidates' skills to during the recruitment process.

 **tip**

Spend time with the person who is leaving, especially if they have been excelling in this role. Ask them to write down their typical daily / weekly / monthly / annual routines.

When you go through this list with them you may well find that there are some things that you didn't even know they did and some things you assumed they did but they don't! It can be quite an eye opener.

Ask them to allocate the percentage of their time spent doing each task. This will not only help you plan your recruiting but will enable you to ensure the job is covered properly before the new person joins.

Analyse what they have said and decide if that is how you want the role to continue. You can use this for the basis of your job specification, adding any other additional duties and responsibilities.

Recruiting for a new vacancy

Of course this could be a new vacancy because your company is expanding, an exciting time for someone to join. Time spent considering the role at this stage will pay off and it will help you focus on what is really needed, how this person will fit in with the rest of the team as well as what their specific duties will involve. It will also ensure that there is no conflict with other staff and that this role does not cross over what they are doing.

brilliant **tip**

If it's a new role you will need to start afresh. Don't try and amend an old job spec for a totally new role, as this will become too confusing.

- Start by looking at the reasons it has been decided to add to the team.

- Decide on what is the overall objective of the role.

- If possible discuss it with the team and anyone else this role will impact on or interface with. It will help you decide on the specific tasks, and the team will feel included; you want them to feel that this person will be an asset, not a threat.

- List the tasks (this does not need to include how internal procedures work as they will be apparent once in the business).

- Put the tasks in priority order with the one that is the most important first.

 brilliant timesaver

All of this need not take very much time but preparation at this stage will pay dividends. It will save you from hiring the wrong person and having to spend time re-recruiting.

Writing the job specification

In large companies the Human Resources team will usually write the job specifications in conjunction with the line manager, so you may be involved in this part of the process or in smaller companies you may need to write one yourself.

More detailed job specifications can include a breakdown of percentage of time spent in each task and how success will be measured.

It is important to compile these as accurately as possible. An employee can refuse to carry out a task you ask them to do, and you cannot discipline anyone for failing to do something, or underperforming, if the task is not included in the job specification.

⤴ brilliant confidence booster

It can be very embarrassing if the candidate asks you a question about the job that you can't answer because you have not considered it. If you have reviewed, rewritten or put together a new job spec then you will have the confidence to answer.

Job specification format

Your company may already have a job specification format, but if not it is worth drawing up one of your own. It need not be complicated but it will be a useful tool throughout the recruitment process and afterwards. It can also form the basis of an assessment once the candidate is hired.

The job specification should be written so that it can be understood both internally and externally, as it is good practice to advertise the role internally, if appropriate, and to share it with the external candidates.

☀ brilliant tip

Do not use company jargon, job titles, process names or anything else that will not be understood by the candidates. A term you use every day with significant meaning in your company, but one that is company-specific, will mean nothing to external candidates. 'Drive to ship', which in one company refers to getting the product to market, will be totally misleading to external candidates.

The job spec can include some or all of the following:

● some brief information about your company
● how the role fits in with the organisation (include an organisation chart if possible)

- the structure of the company
- the structure of the team (if appropriate)
- who the role reports to
- any direct reports
- main function or overall objective of the job
- duties and responsibilities, i.e. the tasks involved and how often, i.e. daily, monthly, annually. Start with the main part of the job first to ensure you have the right emphasis
- a 'cover all' such as 'any other tasks as required by the business'
- measurement of success – by including this in each of the main tasks it will help the candidates understand what they are striving for
- hours of the job / operational times. If you are not giving specific hours then hours the company is open will be useful. Full details will be in the offer letter and contract
- remuneration, i.e. salary and benefits (if appropriate – in some companies these will all be negotiable)
- the candidate specification (see Chapter 2)
- how success in the role will be measured.

Be careful not to include any wording that could be discriminatory. The job specification should not refer to the job holder as 'he' or 'she', and therefore needs to be written neutrally.

> be careful not to include any wording that could be discriminatory

Do not include anything that could imply it can only be done by one sex, such as manual jobs only being done by men.

 **brilliant** timesaver

Use the job spec to brief your recruiters and the candidates, write advertisements, assess CVs and interviewed candidates and circulate internally if appropriate.

Every company's job specification format will be different and there are no right or wrong ways to present it, but the main areas that must be included are detailed below.

Who does this role report to?

It is important to ask:

Q Is the role reporting to the right line manager?

As companies develop it sometimes makes sense to re-assign the reporting line to a more appropriate manager. Discuss this with them and then ensure that they are involved and agree the job specification.

The main function / overall objective

Decide on what the 'overall' or 'main' function of the job is. It should be brief, to the point, and should convey the essence of the role. The specifics of the role will all be related to this.

brilliant examples

For a Facilities Manager this could be: to ensure the smooth and efficient running of the company's facilities.

For a building site manager: to ensure the safe, timely and cost-effective construction / refurbishment of the company's contracts.

Duties and responsibilities

These are the tasks that the job holder is expected to carry out and should include daily, weekly, monthly and annual tasks as well as any that have to be carried out more sporadically.

To compile these, if you have them, you can use the existing job specification updated and amended accordingly or the list of duties the employee who is leaving has compiled that you have reviewed, added to and amended where necessary.

If you are compiling a new job specification, start with what will be the most important or most time-consuming task and work through to the smaller parts. Remember to include all regular tasks, not just daily ones, and any that are more sporadic, for example being responsible for organising fire drills.

Include a last point on the list of tasks / duties such as 'anything else as deemed necessary within the business'.

There may be other situations taking place in your organisation, so once you have your schedule of duties consider the following questions before finalising your job spec:

Q What else do I need to include?

You may be aware of situations such as re-structuring or out-sourcing, etc., which mean that this job must change or have additional or different duties included. Ideally you will let candidates see the finished job spec so ensure these points are included, unless they are still confidential.

Q If the role reports directly to you, is there anything else you need specifically included?

It is difficult to ask employees to take on extra work once they have joined the business, so this is the time to change or expand the job role. Are there any tasks currently covered by other staff that should be included in this role?

 **brilliant** example

Part of your role when you joined the company was ordering and negotiating on the company stationery. Despite several promotions, this task has followed you. Why not make it part of the remit for the new person?

No-one likes to make redundancies but it is even more difficult when it is someone only recently hired. If the role had been reviewed it might have been decided not to hire in the first place. It's also worth considering if there are any alternatives.

Q Could this role be amalgamated?

There may be another role within the organisation that is currently under review which may mean someone can take on all or part of this role, or there may be two or more vacancies which could be combined.

If you are going to amalgamate roles you need to consider if this will work in practice.

---

brilliant do's and don'ts

- Don't try and be too clever and end up combining roles that are too diverse, as you will make it unlikely to find a candidate with experience to cover all the necessary elements.
- Don't combine roles which will mean the candidate has two or more different direct reporting lines. Very few people can manage this situation without some kind of conflict.
- Do ensure that the experience and skills needed for any combined role are possible to find.
- Do consider that a candidate may not have to have all this experience – could they grow or be trained into part of the role?

Remuneration

You may have set salary bands within your business and each job may be already graded with a specific pay range.

If you don't have this or you are recruiting a new vacancy you will have to set the level you want to pay. It's worth comparing what others are paying for similar roles if this is possible. Take a look at websites, advertisements, etc. and discuss this with your recruitment consultants if you are using any.

Remember, your salary may need to tempt someone away from their present role.

Apart from basic salary, think what else you could include such as medical insurance, pension contributions, discounts and so on. There are also companies that specialise in vouchers for different perks. Most of these benefits are taxable so the monetary advantage may not be that great, but their perceived value is high.

In certain sectors it is usual to offer more than the statutory four weeks' holiday and if you are offering less than the norm this will cause a problem. People do not like to give up five weeks' holiday for four. Make sure you are offering what is accepted in your sector or better.

How success in the role will be measured

You may want to include on the job specification the breakdown of how much time is spent on each task so that candidates can see how their time will be structured. This will be a useful guide for your interviews as you can compare what the candidate says they spend most of their time doing with what you need. It will also help identify what are the most important elements of the job and which ones need to be measurable to indicate the new employee's success in the role.

Try and quantify how success in this role will be measured.

 **example**

A retailer is recruiting a store operations director. They have a five-year plan to open ten new stores. Part of the success in this role will be measured by achieving the roll-out plan, turnover of the stores, profitability.

Some larger companies include the use of key performance indicators (KPIs) in their candidate specification, especially if the role has performance-related pay.

brilliant definition

KPIs are the way of measuring success for part of the role. Success in each of these is then related to annual appraisals, grading and often pay awards.

By informing the job holder at the outset how they will be evaluated, you will save disputes and confusion later on. However, if you include KPIs you must adhere to the criteria for appraisals and reviews especially if they are linked to pay awards.

There are some very complex systems for developing these, which may already be set up by your HR department. However, you can introduce simple methods of calculating success.

brilliant example

Salespeople will often have salary related to sales via a commission payment but in some cases they can earn bonuses on profitability, opening of new accounts, opening of new doors, i.e. where an existing customer opens new outlets, the number of cold calls that are made, how well they plan their journeys if they are a sales representative, how many customer visits they make, how well they do on repeat orders, etc. These can all be used as KPIs.

Decide what will be a successful outcome for this job holder and identify how that can be measured. In a call centre this could include the number of calls taken in a period of time, the time spent on each call, the number of calls that had to be followed up, etc.

🔝 brilliant summary

- Take time to review why you are recruiting.

- Consider if you can amalgamate roles or parts of roles.

- Decide if the reporting line is still working.

- Amend, re-write or create a new job spec – even though you are time-short this will save time in the long run.

- Ensure you include all the duties.

- Keep your job specification jargon-free.

CHAPTER 2

Identifying the ideal candidate

Writing the candidate specification

Now that you have reviewed the needs of the business and finalised the job specification, it's time to think about the candidate. What you are about to put together is usually called the 'candidate' or 'person specification', 'candidate profile' or something similar.

brilliant definition

The **candidate specification** identifies what skills and experience the candidates need to have and should match closely with what you have decided are the main elements of the job.

As with the job spec it is important to give this some logical thought, otherwise you may end up employing the person you liked best but who may not be the ideal candidate for the job.

Time spent at this stage – and it needn't take long – will pay off in the end and this, together with the job spec, can also be used as part of your briefing for agencies or advertising. It doesn't need to be detailed but it is useful to have something in writing, especially if others are going to be involved in the interviews – it will ensure that you are all looking for the same qualities. It may also be helpful to discuss it with your fellow interviewers before finalising it.

 **brilliant** timesaver

If other managers are going to be involved in the recruitment process, make sure they agree on the candidate specification before they start interviewing. You really don't want them selecting different candidates for different reasons and then having a debate on what skills and experience are needed!

The candidate specification will help you assess the applicants' details and the interviewees when you meet in person. Generally you can use four main sectors in order to consider the various aspects of their backgrounds and which are the most important elements. For each candidate you will then need to decide how important the sectors are.

- Education.
- Skills.
- Experience.
- Personality.

Skills and personality traits often merge, and some of us, for example, can be natural leaders and therefore think of this as a personality trait while others have learned how to lead and therefore it's a skill. In this context skills should include fields that can be learned, and personality those that are inherent in our nature.

brilliant tip

Hire people because you consider they can do the job and are the best matched candidate, and not because you liked them. Liking them will be an added advantage but it is not a reason to take someone on.

Education

The most easily assessed of these elements is education. Your company may have a policy on, for example, only hiring graduates into certain level jobs.

If there isn't a policy, then consider what you really need. Before you decide on the level or the specific qualifications you are going to ask for, consider *why* you need them and whether they are *really* necessary.

- In some roles this will be obvious. You are not going to recruit a doctor without a medical degree but in non-specialist and non-vocational roles then it is less clear.
- If you think the candidates must have a degree, ask yourself why.
- If it's because you want them to be able to show a good general education, the ability to focus on something for a period of time or other more general reasons, you may be excluding others who have the right experience but for some perfectly valid reason did not go to university.
- However, if you are recruiting for example someone to work in a science-based role you may need them to have a degree as this could be the only way you can validate their knowledge.
- You must be able to justify why you have specified educational qualifications to ensure that you are not being discriminatory in any way. For example, fewer older candidates will have a degree as not so many people went to university at the time

they left school, and by insisting on a degree you could be excluding them. (See Chapter 16, Discrimination.)

● For the same reason don't exclude older style or international qualifications, so for example make sure if you specify GCSE you include 'or equivalent' so that you are not prejudicing more mature candidates who have 'O' Levels.

● Qualifications are not the only measure of intelligence or competence. Is there another way to assess these skills?

 **brilliant example**

You are recruiting for a role in which a major part involves signing off expenses, some of which can be complex. The successful candidate will therefore need to be numerate and have an eye for detail, but do they need to have a qualification such as 'A' Level maths? There are other ways of seeing if they can cope with this situation, so do not exclude good candidates by putting unnecessary requirements in your candidate specification. It may be more appropriate to include a practical task which will assess their ability. (See Chapter 4, Your Recruitment and Selection Process.)

> do not exclude good candidates by putting unnecessary requirements in your candidate specification

When you analyse what you are looking for, in many jobs skills and experience will outweigh the educational needs unless there are specific qualifications for your company or type of work.

However, if you are recruiting junior roles or other roles which you know will attract a high response you may want to use the qualifications as a screening tool with which you can cut numbers down but you will have to ensure that these are justified.

brilliant do's and don'ts

- Do make sure that you are aware of other qualification equivalents, especially older style and international ones.

- Do make sure that the qualification you are demanding is needed to do the job.

- Do try and think of another way of assessing skills.

- Do not include a requirement that is not necessary and therefore potentially discriminatory.

Skills

Many interviewers assess candidates on their experience alone, but it is usually the skills they can bring to you which are most important. Try to identify the skills you need first and then decide what experience will demonstrate these.

Experience in one company doing what sounds a similar job does not automatically mean that the candidate has the correct skills for your role. Job titles often mean different things in different organisations and the emphasis of the role and the way it is managed may bear no relationship to the one you are trying to fill. Try to think what skills you need for your position and then relate that to the types of jobs the candidate could have done.

brilliant example

You are recruiting a customer service clerk to deal with your wholesale clients. Most of the work is on the telephone and you need someone who is proactive and can sell additional product to these customers.

You decide to put as essential 'experience in a customer service role'. One of the candidates has this but they have been dealing directly with consumers

▶

and mainly by letter and email. Although their experience looks a good match, this candidate does not have or cannot demonstrate from their experience that they have the verbal communication or sales skills.

In this profile you need to ask for the candidate to be able to demonstrate verbal communication and sales skills. It is the skills which are important.

If you have a plethora of candidates who fit the bill more closely then you should reject this one. However, if you are short of interesting candidates then you may want to interview them but you need to make sure that you establish if they have these verbal communication skills.

Ask yourself the following question:

ⓠ What *skills* does the candidate need to have?

By going through your job specification and thinking about the situations the job holder will have to deal with, you can identify the skills they will need.

These could be:

- Organisational – their ability to manage their workload, organise projects or events, etc.
- Communication – this may include spoken, written, telephone at all levels but may need specialist skills, for example in a marketing team.
- Management – how they manage their team.
- Decision-making ability.
- Financial – numeracy skills.
- Sales – retail or wholesale – ability to sell new products, increase sales to existing accounts.
- Technical – are their skills in a specific area what you need? – operating machinery through to diagnosing highly specialised mechanical problems.

- Influencing – can they get things done even by those that may not work directly for them?

- Leadership – can they take the lead in different situations and persuade others to follow?

- Team work – ability to work in a team.

- Planning – are they able to plan ahead, work to schedules, etc.?

Try to establish what skills you need for the role you are recruiting and from that decide what experience, how much and in what type of environments you are likely to find candidates who can demonstrate these. Again, if you think you are going to be inundated with responses then you can make these more demanding in order to use them as a selection tool.

 brilliant definition

The term 'selection tool' can be applied to anything you use to enable you to compare candidates for short listing and then for interviewing and ultimately hiring.

Experience

The next stage is to decide what type of experience the applicants will need to have, to be able to demonstrate to you that they do have these skills.

Ⓠ **Do they need to have gained the relevant experience in a similar company or department?**

For example, if you are searching for someone with good administration skills to work in your sales department, does their experience have to be within a similar function or could they have worked in any type of administration?

Q Is there a reason to specify that they MUST have gained their admin experience within a sales department?

They may be customer-facing from day one and therefore this IS essential.

When considering more senior roles you want to hire someone with proven managerial experience.

Q Does this have to be in the same field or could they have managed a team in a totally different type of company?

management skills are transferable: they may not need to work in the same sector

Management skills are transferable: they may not need to work in the same sector.

Q How big a team must they have managed to be able to demonstrate they can manage yours?

Management skills are the same no matter what size the team is, so providing they can demonstrate management skills perhaps they could have managed a different sized team.

Q How much experience should / can I ask for?

Once you have ironed out where their experience needs to come from, think about how much experience they will need. Try to quantify this in terms of what they will need to have done to prove they have the skills for your role. Give this careful thought, as specifying a length of experience is no longer considered good practice. You have to be able to justify why you need it, and if you can't then it can be seen as ageist and prejudiced against people who are too young to have been in the workplace for the length of time you are demanding.

Try to think of it in terms of what they will need to have done to prove they have the skills that are an essential requirement of your vacancy.

🏅 brilliant example

In an executive role which involves setting and overseeing budgets, you may want the successful applicant to have seen through several financial years which will also include years where they have set, monitored and re-evaluated their own budgets. To do this they will have been in a similar role for at least three years, as the first year they will have inherited the budgets, second year will be theirs but it is not until the third year that they will be able to review their own budgets.

Use this as your criterion rather than specifying five years' experience.

If you have considered but dismissed promoting internally, you must have identified a skill missing in your internal candidates. Don't forget to include this in your candidate specification.

🏅 brilliant tip

When recruiting a general manager you may have already dismissed the idea of promoting any of your junior managers because they do not have strong enough presentation skills. Ensure that this need is covered when you put together the candidate specification. It will also help ensure that these junior managers feel they have been treated fairly.

Many of the skills you have identified that your applicants need to have will be covered in one set of experience. A sales manager should be able to demonstrate their sales ability, managerial expertise, communication skill, budgeting know-how, etc. over a period of time, but this can be in just one job.

Personality

Personality can be a very sensitive topic but it may also be an important factor to enable the candidate to deal with different situations. You don't want an extrovert in an analysis role or an introvert in a media role. However, it can be very difficult to quantify for the purposes of the specification and can be very subjective, i.e. what one person considers a confident personality another can see as being difficult.

Try and think of the situations the successful candidate will have to deal with and then decide what type of personality they will need to succeed in them.

● What kind of person will fit well in the team – lively, studious?

● They deal with your customers – outgoing?

● The problems they will deal with are very complex – tenacity?

● The problems are very detailed – eye for detail?

● The solution is not always obvious – analytical?

● The information they deal with is highly sensitive – confidentiality?

● They will have access to cash – honesty?

● There is not always a set process for dealing with problems – initiative?

Importance of each element

As you consider each element, also think about how important each one may be and cross-refer this with the job specification. You can quantify each category by calculating whether each element is 'essential', 'desirable' or 'useful'. This will help you to evaluate candidates both from their curriculum vitae and during the interview.

● Firstly decide on what is 'essential' for the role. This will be education level, skills or experience that the candidate must have to enable them to complete the job. It will include areas that you are not willing or able to train in and it will usually relate to the points in the specification that are the most important parts of the job. If you are to proceed with a candidate they MUST have these essential elements.

● Other candidate features may not be essential but they will be desirable. You would not dismiss a candidate from consideration simply for not having these, but they will help you compare and select candidates. They do not have to have these qualities to be able to do the job, but they will assist the candidate greatly.

● Thirdly are those elements that are useful. These are parts of the candidate's make-up that will simply give them added value, and again can be used to select between candidates.

brilliant example

Your company works in the Spanish market so you are thinking of hiring a Spanish speaker, but is this an 'essential', 'desirable' or 'useful' skill?

If your company works exclusively with Spanish companies where your contacts do not speak English, or the role will cover this specific market, added to which cold-calling new prospects is involved, then speaking and writing Spanish fluently is ESSENTIAL.

If your company works with Spanish customers most of whom speak some English, then speaking Spanish is DESIRABLE, although this could be conversational rather than fluent.

If your company's Spanish contacts all speak English but it would help to build the relationships if someone can have a brief conversation with them in their native tongue, then Spanish will be USEFUL.

Although the aim is to find a candidate with all of the essential, desirable and useful skills and experience it is not always possible. Compromise on the useful elements first, as these are 'add-ons', then the desirable ones, but try not to compromise at all on the essential. If you compromise on the essential it will leave you with a training need that you had not allowed for or a candidate who is going to take much longer than anticipated to grow into the role.

Before finalising the candidate specification you may want to 'adjust' it according to the level of difficulty there may be in finding suitable candidates.

How difficult is it going to be to fill this role?

The candidate profile should reflect this by being more flexible and less demanding if it's a difficult role likely to have only a few responses. You may be able to do this by keeping an open mind on where they gained their experience; it could be in any type of company, not just one in the same area as yours.

If it's an easy role to fill with lots of potential candidates, by making the criteria tougher you can immediately reject some of them but don't make the criteria so tough that you end up recruiting someone who is over-qualified and therefore expecting more from the job.

Make sure you pitch your candidate specification at the right level. Do not make it so demanding that no candidate can possibly reach the criteria or alternatively so open that anyone could apply.

Finally, ensure that all of your criteria are necessary for the job and that you have not included anything that could be discriminatory. For example, insisting on written fluency in English when there is no written work in the job may help you screen candidates but it could be seen as discriminatory.

🡵 brilliant summary

- Do not use terminology the candidates will not know or understand because it is company jargon.
- Do be realistic about the person you are seeking: don't ask for so much that you will never find a candidate.
- Concentrate on skills rather than experience.
- Decide on the essential aspects that you cannot compromise on and others in the desirable and useful categories that you can.
- Include the candidate profile with the job specification and give it to candidates to help them understand your requirements.
- Ensure you have not included any criteria which could be prejudicial to certain groups.

CHAPTER 3

Sourcing candidates

Where do you find the best applicants?

The next decision is where to source your applicants. The main factor in this choice is likely to be costs, so you first need to determine what your recruitment budget is. Then you will need to consider how this budget will be best used.

brilliant tip

It is worth monitoring what response you get from each consultancy or the media that you use so that you have some information to base your decisions on next time you recruit.

Internet-based advertising is now one of the most widely-used media for recruiting but some of the more traditional methods are still worth considering, as is the use of a third party such as a recruitment consultancy or advertising agency.

There are pros and cons with each method so it is a matter of deciding which will be the most successful and cost-effective for you.

The main media for sourcing candidates are as follows:

- Your company website.
- Recruitment websites.

- Advertising in traditional media – local press, national press and trade magazines.
- Recruitment consultancies.
- Retained assignments.
- Advertising agencies.
- Radio advertising.
- Job centres.

Company website

This can work particularly well in large, well-known companies. Many people actively looking to change jobs will automatically search the websites of their competitors and organisations they are already aware of to ascertain if they have any appropriate vacancies.

For smaller, less well-known companies this will be less productive as prospective candidates will not be automatically drawn to your website. However, it is still good practice to advertise your vacancies, especially if your company operates an open style of management where you want your present staff to be aware of what is going on. It can also be a good public relations exercise, especially if it's a new vacancy because of expansion.

If you are going to start using your own website it is easier for the applicants if they can send their details directly from the web page. The cost implications of this may outweigh the benefits for smaller companies so the alternative is to make sure the advertisement clearly states how to apply.

Company website pros and cons – the pros
- Low cost as the site is already operational.
- Candidates know your company and want to work for you.
- World-wide coverage.
- Good PR exercise.

Company website pros and cons – the cons

- Only works for well-known companies.

- Executives are less likely to respond, especially if they are currently employed. There is still reluctance amongst senior employees, some older ones and those in more formal environments, to apply online because of concerns over confidentiality.

- It works better if candidates can email directly from the web page but this will involve further costs.

Recruitment website

Recruitment websites have been the biggest change in sourcing candidates in the last few years. As more people have had internet access at home and in the office, these websites have mushroomed. It is now easy for employees, and very annoying for employers, to search for a new job while sitting at their desk having lunch!

The main problem is how to decide which site to try. You need to research the sites available to see which ones will suit your needs. You want a site that is advertising similar

> it is now easy for employees to search for a new job while at their desk having lunch!

jobs to the one you are recruiting for so that you know you will be attracting candidates with the right background.

Some sites cover all disciplines, while others are more specialised. Rather than going by what the sites claim to cover, take a look at the actual jobs they are advertising. When you are going through each site, ask yourself the following:

Q Are they advertising a similar job and a similar level to yours?

If you are looking for a middle management level candidate then ensure there are other vacancies at that level. If your advert is amongst more junior ones it will be lost or it will put the candidates off. Make sure the website can attract the right candidates for you.

Ⓠ Do they cover your market sector?

Both generalist and the more specialist websites break the vacancies down into sector headings. It can be difficult to decide where your particular role will fit and may mean you have to pay to go into more than one sector heading. Find a site that has an obvious place for your advertisement to go.

Ⓠ What geographical area do you want to attract candidates from?

You may have a similar difficulty with location and the way the areas are broken down on the website. Ensure this is going to work for you.

Ⓠ What are the costs?

You are usually charged per vacancy, but there are better deals if you are going to be a regular user and/or have more than one job to advertise. When comparing costs, also check how long your advert will appear and what you will pay if you decide to extend this period. You should also be able to get an introductory discount, especially if you can promise more jobs to come.

It is also possible to pay to search the CVs held on the website. This is useful if you are constantly recruiting but, for one-off roles, the chances of coming across the right person for you at the right time are remote.

Recruitment websites – the pros

- Low costs.
- Easy access for potential applicants.
- CVs emailed directly to you.

Recruitment websites – the cons

- Senior executives less likely to apply.
- It is not always possible to find the right category or geographical area for your role.
- Anyone can apply as there is no screening of applicants.

Advertising in traditional media

Because of the ease for your candidates to view and apply online, make sure that the media you choose also include coverage on their website or an option to pay extra for this. You will lose candidates who do not read newspapers even when looking for a new job, simply because they assume that all jobs are advertised online.

For executive roles it is still the best option, as older and senior candidates respond better to press advertising even if they see the ad and then go through to the website.

Have a look through newspapers and magazines that you think will be appropriate for your advertisement.

Are there jobs similar to yours being advertised?

What circulation does this medium have?

What type of people is it aimed at?

What geographical coverage does it have?

What size of advert will you need to make it stand out on the page?

There are three types of publication to consider.

- National press is expensive but if you need countrywide coverage for a generalist role or one where you will consider applicants from any sector, then this is the only place you can advertise. Because of the cost you should only consider national press for senior executive roles or where you are recruiting a group of people with a similar background to join as trainees, for example. If you are looking for a senior candidate but from a specific sector, then using a trade magazine is more cost-effective.

● Local press is a good way to recruit junior staff already living in your catchment area. Newspapers selling across major conurbations, the city dailies, can still be expensive so consider if there is a smaller, more localised publication you could use.

● Trade press can be used to attract candidates that you have specified must have experience from your trade sector, and will give you national coverage. It will also reach subscribers worldwide and will be less expensive than using a national paper.

Your advertisement should:

● Include your company name and logo, if you have one, and reflect your company profile.

● Be written clearly and jargon-free.

● Contain a brief outline of the job.

● Detail any key elements, such as extensive travel, that candidates may not want to do and therefore there will be no point in applying.

● Detail the essential skills the candidate will need (avoid putting length of experience in case this is discriminatory – see Chapter 16, Discrimination).

● Avoid any discriminatory wording such as 'to join a young, lively team' which will be discriminatory against older applicants (see Chapter 16, Discrimination).

● State location.

● State salary.

● Detail how to apply.

Some local advertisements may only be linage ads, where you pay per line so there will not be space for much wording or logos. Check how these adverts appear, and copy the format. The first word is usually the job title, and then the minimum you need to include will be company name, salary and how to apply (telephone number / email address is usually sufficient).

You will need to research costs and obtain a rate card from each publication you are considering.

brilliant definition

The **rate card** is a list of advertisement sizes, the cost for an eighth, quarter, half, full page and the amount per column centimetre. (If you look at the adverts in the publication you will see that some run across the width of one column and you pay for that per centimetre down.) The rate card will also include deadline dates for booking space and for sending the copy.

If you intend to use one publication for regular adverts or a prolonged campaign, ask for a discount.

If you need to advertise but prefer some of the leg work taken out of it, then consider using an advertising agency (see below).

Advertising in traditional media – the pros

- Coverage – national and trade press will be seen nationally and by some readers internationally.
- National press and city dailies will generate a large response which will be useful if you are recruiting several candidates for the same job.
- Trade press will ensure applicants only from your market sector.

- Local press is inexpensive.
- Local press will ensure the candidates are from your catchment area.

Advertising in traditional media – the cons
- You will need to research costs.
- Cost – national, trade and some city dailies can be expensive.
- Cost – localised publications are inexpensive but have limited exposure.
- Response – advertisements in both national and city dailies can generate large responses and you will need to acknowledge receipt of details.
- Writing the advertisement takes time and skill.
- You will need to get the advertisement typeset – i.e. put into the correct layout for printing (some publications will do this for you for a fee).
- You will need to book space in plenty of time.
- You will have to deal with the rejected applicants.

Advertising agencies

Advertising agencies are a useful tool if you are recruiting without a human resource team. Use an agency that specialises in recruitment advertising, not one that is product-based.

Advertising agencies can offer you the following:

- advice on the best media, including publications and radio, to use for your particular vacancy
- they will have all the rate cards for all the relevant publications to hand
- can advise on the size and format of your advertisement
- will write the advert for you
- will have it typeset (put into the correct layout for printing)
- will place it with the publication.

They make their money from the discounts they are given by the publications they advertise in so there is no charge for this service but they will, of course, be keen for you to take as large a space as possible. You will have to pay for the cost of the advert in full and for the typesetting, but these are costs you would have if you were doing it yourself. The advantage is that they are taking away some of the time-consuming administration for you and they are expert copy writers.

Some will also offer to do some of the screening for you but any other service they provide will be charged for.

Make sure you give them a detailed brief, not only on the role you are recruiting but on your company, its values and culture. Give them a copy of the job and candidate descriptions.

Advertising agencies – the pros
- Their services are free.
- Offer advice on where to advertise.
- Will have rate cards to hand.
- Can expertly write your advert.
- Will organise typesetting.
- Take away a lot of the admin such as booking space, etc.

Advertising agencies – the cons
- You will need to spend time briefing them on your company and the job, to ensure they pitch the advertisement copy correctly.
- Their service is limited to advertising so you will still have to screen CVs and conduct interviews.

Recruitment agencies / consultancies

Recruitment agencies and consultancies often get a bad press. Candidates looking for work will complain that they didn't find them a job but then they forget that the recruitment consultancy is actually working for their client companies and is a free service to applicants. Employers complain that they sent them the wrong candidates but very often they have not briefed the recruitment consultant properly.

Of course there are good and bad consultancies and consultants, but if you take the time to work with them and brief them fully they can be very useful. If you are recruiting on your own without any HR back-up the services they offer can considerably cut down the time you spend recruiting.

Most work on a success-only fee. That is, you will only pay when you hire someone. For executive roles it may be appropriate to consider a retained assignment – see below.

You can cherry-pick the services that they offer from the following list:

- Providing you with candidates they have continually been sourcing via their own advertising, internet, and speculative applicants so that you don't need to advertise directly.
- A data bank of candidates, so for many roles they will be able to supply interviewees very quickly.
- For more complex or senior roles, advertising on your behalf. This can include your company logo and you will usually be asked to pay for this or pay a percentage of the cost – make sure you have the final sign-off on the advertisement.
- Dealing with the response from the advertising.
- Dealing with rejected candidates at all stages.
- Headhunting – where someone is approached directly for your role. This has been traditionally carried out by the large international recruitment consultancies working on behalf of clients seeking senior executives. However, due to a shortfall of candidates in some job categories even at quite junior levels it has become much more commonplace and is carried out by most recruiters.

- Advice on pay rates.

- Advice on benefits.

- Conducting the first interview (do insist that all of the candidates you are interviewing have been seen in person by the recruitment consultant. For junior roles this may mean that they have interviewed them generally but not for your specific role. For more senior roles you need to insist that they are interviewed specifically for your job).

- Briefing candidates on your company and the job.

- Setting up the interviews.

- Following up interview feedback and setting up further interviews.

- Taking up references (usually only when specifically asked to do so).

- Negotiating the offer and start-date on your behalf.

- Some agencies will even write your job and candidate specification for higher-level positions. Not all consultancies will offer this service but once they have worked with you for some time they should be prepared to and you should feel confident that they can.

brilliant tip

Recommendation is the best way to source a recruitment consultancy. Try asking at any networking groups you attend and you will also find out which ones not to use.

If you are headhunted and you felt that the approach worked well, keep a note of the consultant's name and contact details.

Review any advertisements for similar roles to the one you are recruiting and see if any of those are being handled via a consultancy.

Finding the right recruitment company for you is difficult as there are now so many. There are three main types: generalists that will handle any job in any sector, job category specialists i.e. marketing, sales, finance, etc. and sector specialists, i.e. retail, fast moving consumer goods and so on.

Which is most important for you, finding a candidate from your sector of the market or, providing they have the right skills, can they come from any sector?

▶ brilliant example

Your company imports gifts which you have sold via the internet but you are now planning to open your own retail stores. You are replacing your finance manager. Can they come from any sector, providing they have the financial skills, or will it make more sense to go to a consultancy specialising in retail?

Decide on two or three possibilities and then follow the plan below:

- Meet them face to face.
- Plan the meeting. Treat it like an interview – what do you want to know from them and what information do you want to give them?
- Ask what type of companies they work for.
- Ask for examples of candidates they have placed in similar jobs to yours.
- Give them as much information as you can, including details on company culture, the type of people that fit in well.
- Give them copies of the job and candidate specification.
- Give them deadlines – when do you want to interview?
- Make sure both parties are aware of who is paying any candidates' expenses. You should not be asked to pay any

until you meet the candidates unless there are particular circumstances, and then the consultant should take your advice before agreeing to pay anything.

- Ask them to discuss all candidates with you before booking them in to see you.
- Make sure they are not discussing your top level salary when a lower one will suffice.

brilliant example

You are recruiting a store manager with a salary range of £30 – 40,000 per annum plus a company bonus which last year paid 15% of annual salary. You want to hire the best candidate and you want them to feel they have got a good offer but you do not want to pay more than is necessary. If the candidates are told the salary is between £30 and 40,000 their expectations are immediately raised to £40,000 despite the fact that for some £35,000 would have been attractive.

Recruitment fees are usually based on a percentage of the first year's basic salary or salary package and can be between 10 and 35% depending on the level of the job. Make sure you understand what is included as the package – this can include an allowance for the company car, health care, pension, commission, bonuses and any other perks.

There will also be some kind of money back guarantee should the person leave. This is usually worked out on a sliding scale so the longer they work for you before they leave, the less you will be paid as a rebate.

This is all negotiable. The percentage can be reduced if you are briefing on more than one vacancy, or you could ask for a special introductory fee, or offer to pay more quickly for a discount. You may prefer to have a set fee so that you can budget more easily. Try to ensure that you are only paying on the basic salary without any add-ons for cars, etc.

You can also negotiate on the rebate terms should the candidate leave. If you have a three-month probationary period it is not unreasonable to assume that this will be covered. Some companies will also offer a straightforward free replacement should the candidate leave within a set period. If the consultant is sure they can do a good job for you they should be prepared to offer flexibility here.

Recruitment consultancies – the pros
- The main reason to use a recruitment consultant is to save time on
  - writing and placing ads
  - dealing with advert responses
  - dealing with rejected applicants
  - conducting first interviews
  - setting up your interviews.
- They will give you feedback after your interview which will be useful in deciding who to take to the next stage.
- Can give you advice on salary levels in the market and on your offer.
- Can negotiate on your behalf.

Recruitment consultancies – the cons
- Costs are relatively high but if you calculate the time you will spend sourcing candidates directly through advertising, writing and placing the advertisement, taking the response, screening the CVs and shortlisting for first interview it becomes much more reasonable.
- Candidates will be sent on other interviews via the recruitment consultancy so competition can be high.
- Finding a recruitment consultant that you trust can be time-consuming.

Retained assignments – headhunting

The larger or more specialised consultancies will want you to work with them on a retained assignment basis for executive recruiting.

 brilliant definition

A retained assignment is paid for in three stages. The first part will be due immediately and is a non-refundable retainer, the second at the stage where you conduct first interviews, usually referred to as the shortlist stage, and the third on the start date.

The overall fee will be based on the annual salary package and at this level is likely to include any significant benefits such as bonuses, cars, etc. with an estimated third of the overall fee paid at each of the first two stages and the remainder paid at stage three. Fees are generally 30% or more. If you cancel the assignment for any reason you will lose the retainer, and if you have interviewed then the shortlist stage fee must also be paid. As with all other conditions, all of this can be negotiated as necessary.

With a retained assignment the services you have will include all of those for a success-only search but you should get a more detailed service from your consultant. You will be dealing with a senior consultant who will interview in depth for your specific role and will headhunt for you.

This will enable you to work with the consultant to target potential individuals within other companies that you want approached on your behalf. These potential candidates may already be known to you or your recruiter or be identified by research carried out by the consultancy. These are candidates who are not necessarily looking to move, so the recruiter you work with needs to be skilled at making the approach, getting the candidate interested and taking it to the next stage.

This is also useful if you need to keep the recruitment confidential as they can work up to the point that you interview before revealing who your company is.

The main advantage of using this process is that your interviewees should be very closely matched to your role and the recruiter has an obligation to 'get it right' as you have already paid them upfront. An additional benefit is that candidates on a retained assignment shortlist are not shortlisted for other jobs by that consultant so you will have less competition for good candidates.

The disadvantages are that they may ultimately decide not to move, they have to be handled with great confidentiality as you have approached them, and you may have considered a too-limited spectrum of candidates. If someone is doing a similar role to yours in another company and not actively looking, are they really going to change companies?

Retained assignments – the pros
- Targeted headhunt will be included so the candidates will closely match your needs.
- The consultant will be more experienced.
- They will conduct interviews in more depth.
- Confidentiality can be maintained.
- You have paid money upfront so the consultant is committed to finding you the right person.

Retained assignments – the cons
- Headhunted candidates are not necessarily looking to move and may be more likely to withdraw during the interview process.
- Costs are high, but again consider how much of your time will be spent on sourcing candidates if you do it yourself.
- You will have to pay money upfront which is non-refundable.

Radio advertising

Radio advertising can reach a vast audience, with almost 350 commercial radio stations in Britain and some, such as Heart, having audiences of 7.2 million. Because there is now such a choice with different stations attracting different listeners it is possible to target your audience more successfully. You can also be area-specific as there are over 300 local radio stations, or keep it wider with the 20-plus regional and national ones.

Unless you have vast in-house resources it will be easier to use the services of an advertising agency to set up your advertising campaign. They work in the same way for radio advertising as they do with traditional publications, and take a percentage from the medium you are using so they will not charge you for their services. They will have facts and figures to hand so can advise you on what type of listeners each station attracts, the audience numbers, the area it covers, the cost of airtime. They should also have the expertise to get the advertisement produced for you.

The main drawback is that it is an expensive way to advertise. You have to pay for airtime and for the production of your advert. It is worth considering if you are recruiting a large team or for a specific event and need junior or unskilled candidates. Senior candidates are unlikely to respond to this type of medium.

You will also need to have the resources, to cope with the response, as this is likely to be a phone-in application.

Radio advertising – the pros
- There is now a good choice of stations so you can target your audience.
- There are a lot of local stations so you can be area-specific.
- It is good PR for your company to be heard on radio.
- Speed – you will get immediate responses.
- You will get a good number of responses if it is for junior or unskilled roles.

Radio advertising – the cons

- It is expensive and only worth considering if you are recruiting a lot of staff in the same role.

- Unless you are running a sustained campaign, the impact is short-lived. Once the advert has been heard the listener cannot go back to it as they can with a newspaper or website.

- You will need in-house resources to cope with the response, which is usually by telephone.

Job centres

The cheapest form of recruiting is via your local job centre. It's free and there may even be a financial incentive to recruit someone who has been claiming Job Seeker's Allowance for over six months.

> the cheapest form of recruiting is via your local job centre

Their facilities have greatly improved over the last few years and they are now much more modern and more like a high-street recruitment agency; services to employers have also improved and you can create and manage jobs online.

If you are recruiting for junior or unskilled roles this can often be the most cost-effective way and if this is likely to be an ongoing need in your business it is worth developing a good working relationship with your local centre.

It is far less productive for senior roles, as very few are advertised in the job centres and therefore executive candidates are not likely to even think to search for their new job there.

Job centres – the pros

- It's free.
- You can create and review your jobs online.

- For junior, semi-skilled or unskilled jobs you will get candidates quickly.

- Your jobs will be advertised internationally.

Job centres – the cons

- Your job will generally only be seen by unemployed people.

- Applicants are under pressure to be seen to be applying for jobs, often resulting in unsuitable applicants.

- It will only attract candidates for junior, semi-skilled or unskilled jobs.

- There is little or no matching of candidates to jobs, so anyone can apply for your vacancy.

- Middle managers upwards, even though they are signing on, generally will not apply for jobs via a job centre.

- Your job will only be seen by a limited number of people.

- They are not working for you so you cannot expect them to screen candidates on your behalf.

How do you want your candidates to apply?

Whichever way you decide to source your candidates, you will also need to decide how you want them to apply to you or how you want the recruitment consultant to submit them to you. The four main ways are via an emailed CV, a hard copy CV, by telephone call or by calling to request an application form.

The most usual is an emailed CV as this is quickest and easiest for both applicants and employer. You should acknowledge all CVs received but this can usually be set up automatically on your email system. The shortlisted candidates can be easily circulated and shared with others involved in the recruitment. However, some companies still prefer hard copy CVs.

Telephone applications are useful if you are looking for someone urgently or the role involves telephone communication skills. You should have some screening questions ready, as outlined in Chapter 4, Your Recruitment and Selection Process.

In larger organisations it may be necessary to apply using an application form. This can cause delay if applicants have to ring to request that a form is sent or emailed to them and you then have to wait for them to send it back. It will be quicker to ask them to complete it at interview stage or at least to fill in the sections not covered on their CV. The advantage of an application form is that it is easier to compare one candidate to another.

Whichever route you select, make sure the method and relevant contact details are on all your advertisements.

brilliant summary

- Set a recruitment budget and then decide how best to use it.
- If you have a company website, use it to advertise your vacancies.
- Ensure that you are advertising in the right place.
- Make sure your advertisements include everything you need.
- Make sure your advertisements and your brief to advertising or recruitment consultancies are non-discriminatory.
- Select the best advertising or recruitment consultancy for your company and job.

CHAPTER 4

Your recruitment and selection process

How to decide who to interview and select

Before the curriculum vitae arrive you need to decide what process you want the candidates to go through, including who they will need to meet, at what stage, and in what time frame. For junior roles this may be one interview with you or the line manager but the more complex the role you are recruiting, the more complex the process is likely to have to be.

Plan this now. It's always difficult to co-ordinate diaries so the more notice you can give the interviewers and interviewees the better, you will be able to let the candidates know the process and ensure any recruitment consultants or advertising agencies involved are working to your schedule.

Plan your recruitment timetable up to and including the proposed start date for the new employee, allowing for their notice period, which can be six months or even longer for senior executives. You will then know how long you will need to cover the role until the new person starts, and can also begin considering what sort of induction you will need to organise and whether the relevant staff are in the business at that time.

> plan your recruitment timetable up to and including the proposed start date for the new employee

 **tip**

Book interview times in your diary and the diaries of any others involved at this point so that there is not a problem with availability later. You may also need to book interview rooms. This will also avoid interviewers trying to squeeze interviews in because of a shortage of diary time.

Consider the following when planning your recruitment process:

- The process of selection must be the same for all candidates to ensure they are all treated equally. This will help you assess them in a uniform way and will ensure that none of them can think they have been discriminated against because they were put through a different process. (For example, if you consider that one of your candidates may not have an adequate level of written English you may decide to ask them to complete a written test. If you do not ask all of the others to complete the same test it could be construed as discriminatory. If written English is important then you will be better giving all the candidates the same test and treating them all equally.)

- It is also good practice to have more than one person involved in each stage if possible, to ensure that no individual biases are prevalent.

- Who needs to meet the candidates? The obvious ones will be their line manager and a member of the Human Resources team if you have one. You may also want to include other managers who will be working closely with them or someone from their peer group.

The recruitment or selection process can include some or all of the following, and there may be other parts in the process unique to your company:

- Shortlisting from application form or curriculum vitae.
- Shortlisting from telephone response.
- Telephone interview.
- First interview.
- Second interview.
- Subsequent interview(s).
- Practical task(s).
- Psychometric and other tests.
- Trial.
- Assessment centres.
- Right to work.
- References.
- Police check.
- Medical.
- Offer.

You need to decide which of these stages you need to enable you to identify the candidate that most closely matches your criteria and will fit best into your organisation. If you are using a recruitment consultancy then you should be able to go straight to the first interview stage as they will have pre-selected the candidates for you.

Decide on the ideal numbers of candidates you are aiming to have at each stage. This may change, depending on the number of responses you receive. The optimum number you want to include for first interview may be six but only four met your criteria, or you could have more than you need but can't select down further.

Shortlisting from the CVs or application forms

The CVs have now arrived in your in-box or on your desk so the next stage of your recruitment is to select who to interview.

brilliant tip

If you are using several different kinds of sources or more than one of any kind, internet advertising, recruitment consultants and so on, logging where the largest and best response came from will help you evaluate these sources next time you recruit.

The first thing to do is to create a log in order to record who has applied. Include:

- Name.
- Contact number.
- Source.
- Each stage of your process.
- Outcome.
- Keep on file.

At every stage of your process make a note of whether or not you are including each candidate and then the outcome of that stage, including rejections and when they are sent. Not only will this help you keep tabs on what is happening to each candidate: it will enable you to deal with any queries quickly and easily.

Some candidates may not be appropriate for your current recruitment needs but you may want to keep them on file for other opportunities that may be coming up. Let them know this and make sure they are filed where they can be easily contacted when you need them.

If you have asked for response via email but you have also received hard copies, or vice versa, it is worth asking the candidate to re-submit so that all the responses are filed in the same format; it is also worth noting those who can't follow simple instructions.

The following guidelines will help you select who to take to the next stage:

- Read through the job specification and then the candidate profile.

- Make a note of the essential criteria.

- Read through the covering note – does it include any information that you asked for?

- Read through the CVs to establish which have the 'essential' qualifications, skills, and experience.

- How many of the desirable and useful criteria do they have?

- Highlight any CVs that you are not sure about because the information is ambiguous or you are uncertain about what they have been doing, etc. These may be worth calling to clarify these points.

- Have you got the optimum number for your next stage? If you have too many, then you need to screen further by establishing which have some or all of the 'desirable' criteria.

- If you still need to screen further, then use the 'useful' criteria.

brilliant tip

Using a points system for marking or grading CVs can be helpful, especially if more than one person is involved in the screening. For example, allocate five points for each essential criterion, two for every desirable one and one for each useful one.

If you have a poor response, either too few or not the right calibre, do not be tempted to compromise as you will end up hiring someone who will need a lot more training than you originally planned for or who is just not capable of doing the job. Review your sources and then try another route. It will save time in the long run – hiring the wrong candidate is even more time-consuming.

Shortlisting from telephone response

If you are recruiting junior level staff then you may have asked for your initial response to an advert to be by telephone. This can work particularly well if you are short of time and need to start interviews immediately, or you can use it as a way to test telephone communication skills.

Decide on some brief selection questions you can ask that will help you assess if you should call that person for interview.

What are the most important criteria these candidates need to have?

If you are recruiting temporary staff it may be the dates of availability that are crucial or the ability to do a night shift.

Make sure that the person who is taking the response is fully briefed, has a list of questions and is aware of how to decide who to book in. Remember to give them interview times too.

brilliant tip

You will need to book interviews for the next day if possible. Applicants responding in this way have a very high 'no show' rate if the interviews are more than a couple of days away.

Telephone interview

Your first interview could be a telephone interview rather than face to face, as this can prove useful especially if:

- You have a large response and it is difficult to cut the numbers down on the information you have.
- You have candidates in other countries/locations.

- You are not on the premises so by telephone interviewing you can keep up the momentum rather than having to wait for your return.

> your first interview could be a telephone interview rather than face to face

- Telephone communication skills are an essential part of the job.

 brilliant timesaver

Telephone interviews can be more focussed and therefore much shorter than first face-to-face interviews and therefore save time.

Plan what you want to ask. You may want them to talk through their current or last job, or you may have specific questions to ask related to your candidate profile and you can use some of the questions in Part Two for this.

Call the candidate and introduce yourself and explain that you want to set up a telephone interview. Bear in mind that they may be at work when you speak to them. Outline the points you want to cover and give them an idea of how long this will take. Arrange a suitable time when they will be able to speak to you freely and try and have a landline number to call them on.

Telephone interviewing – the pros and cons

- Saves time – the actual interview will be shorter than a face-to-face one.
- Can speed up the process – putting interview schedules together can be difficult especially at short notice, whereas it will be much easier to set up telephone interviews in the evening or weekend.

- Other countries – if the candidates are a long way away or in a different country this will be much easier to organise and you will not have the issue of travelling costs to consider.
- Observe how they come across on the phone – this is now such an important part of so many jobs but it is often not tested during the interview process.
- You do not get visual response.
- You can't read their body language.

Telephone interviews can be an effective screening tool but they cannot replace the face-to-face interview.

First interview

After going through one or more of the above, you should now have your shortlist for first interview.

The first interview should be to find out more general information about the candidate so that you can assess them alongside your criteria in your candidate specification. The aim is to have enough information to assess the candidate and decide who to take to the next stage, and should cover:

- What type of company they work in .
- More details about their current and previous jobs.
- Reasons for leaving.
- Reasons for applying.
- Practicalities such as travelling or re-location.

It is worth covering some of the more practical issues such as travelling to work for more junior candidates and re-location where appropriate. These issues can often be the cause of offers not being accepted.

If you are aiming to attract candidates from across the country or internationally, you will need to offer them a re-location package. This should be included in your recruitment budget, and details are given in Chapter 15, The Offer.

Second and subsequent interviews

Second and further interviews are not always necessary, so consider carefully what the purpose of these will be. If they are not planned they can all too easily end up with a repeat of the first interview. Reasons for second interviews can include:

- You need to ask more in-depth questions that you didn't cover in the first interview.
- The candidates need to meet other people in your organisation.
- There is a practical task or some form of testing for them to complete.
- The candidates, even junior ones, need to have a sense of achievement if you offer them the job.
- You simply cannot decide between two or more candidates.

If they are meeting other individuals who were not present at the first interview make sure the other interviewers know what areas you have covered so they are not repeating your line of questions. Highlight to them points that they need to probe, and explain why.

brilliant tip

If there are several people involved in the interview process it may be quicker to interview together either in pairs or as a selection panel. You need to make sure that you have assessed the candidate well in order to invite them to this stage, otherwise you could be wasting not just your time but several other people's.

Working in pairs can work well, for example a line manager and a representative from human resources.

▶ brilliant example

If you are the line manager and you are interviewing with someone from HR, the obvious division of questions will be that you could be the one asking questions about their company and job while HR delve into reasons for leaving, future plans, re-location, etc.

Panel interviews only work at senior levels as they are too daunting for junior candidates. The difficulty is usually making sure the people you need are all available.

If you decide on either of these make sure that interviewers and panellists are fully briefed on what you are looking for and find a way to divide the questioning. Agree on who will take the lead in the meeting.

These joint interviews or panels can work very well if they are planned but are disastrous if they are not, with no-one being clear who is asking what.

Practical task(s)

a practical task can often show you much more clearly what a candidate is capable of

As part of the recruitment process you may want to include a practical task. They can often show you much more clearly what a candidate is capable of, how they cope under pressure and how they handle different situations. They can be used for all levels and can be as simple or as complex as the job role demands.

- Practical tasks should be based around your 'essential needs' and should be designed to allow the candidate to demonstrate their skills in a particular area.
- They should not include technology that the candidate is unfamiliar with, unless the task is designed to evaluate their grasp of new technology.
- The format and content must be clear.
- Length of time the task will take should be given if appropriate.
- Tell the candidate what's available / what they need to bring, e.g. laptop.
- Explain what points you are looking for and how they will be assessed.
- Give details of who will be at the meeting.
- The same information should be passed in the same way to each candidate, including any 'tips' that you may want them to use. For example you may want them to understand that you are an informal company and they should be aware of this when doing the task.

The types of task will vary for each job and each company and should be included only if they are going to help identify if the candidate has a particular skill and at what level.

brilliant tip

Practical tasks work brilliantly providing they have an obvious link to the role you are recruiting. If you can't think of an immediately obvious practical task it probably means that it is not appropriate to include in this recruitment process.

The possible tasks for interview range from numeracy and finance through to manual dexterity.

Numeracy and finance

Earlier we looked at a situation where you are recruiting for a role in which a major part involves signing off expenses, some of which can be complex. The successful candidate will therefore need to be numerate and have an eye for detail but they do not necessarily need to have a qualification such as 'A' Level maths. Try asking them to check through several genuine expenses forms to identify any mistakes in a set time. This will demonstrate if they have an eye for detail, ability to spot numeric discrepancies, and speed.

For senior employees use actual budgets, P&L accounts or similar appropriate documents and ask relevant questions about them.

Written English

Replying to customers via email is a large part of this role, so good written business English is essential.

The task could be to give the candidates several emails to reply to, but remember they do not know how your company operates so you will need to give them an outline of what should be included in their reply. You are testing their written English, not their knowledge of your company procedures. If time is an important factor in this role then give them a set time to complete the task.

Here you are looking for common sense, courtesy, the right tone, a clear answer, a timeline and an acceptable level of English.

Presentation skills

Interview tests for sales managers, for example, have different priorities, so design your task to reflect the skills you are trying to assess. In this instance it is presentation skills that are key to the role. You will need to brief these candidates beforehand, including details on the product and the customer they will be meeting.

Set the scene by telling them that you have made an appointment with an existing customer that you have sold into for some time but you now want to sell product at a higher price point. 'Prepare and present a sales presentation. Please indicate what assumptions you have made before you start your presentation. You may use any form you wish but please let us know in advance if you need any equipment. Ashley Standish, our general manager and Kirsty Massoud, sales director, will be at the presentation.'

From this you will be able to assess their presentation skills and you will also have an indication of their ability to understand and interpret instructions, influencing skills, capacity to think on their feet, and how they react under pressure.

Make sure those at the meeting are prepared to ask questions.

Selling skills

The above does not specifically test sales skills, so to assess this you will need a different task.

You need to forewarn your candidates that they will be asked to do a role-play of a selling situation. Decide if you need to brief them beforehand or on the day. What would happen in your company?

Brief the candidate on the product and the customer and then ask them to sell the product to the customer. Explain that they need to close the deal and get an order.

Sales skills are about finding out the customer needs and then matching what you have, product or services, to those requirements. You are looking for someone who is not afraid to ask questions and who can then identify the unique features of the product and match them to what the customer is looking for. Negotiation is also key to sales so in this role-play you can gauge how well they negotiate and whether they can put together a deal that both parties are happy with. If they have bowed on price perhaps they have gained by agreeing a quick payment period.

If the role is more negotiating than sales, then put them straight into the end negotiation situation.

Visual or creative skills

These skills lend themselves to practical tasks. Some are obvious. The portfolio of work presented by a fashion designer might be very interesting, but you are not sure if they can adapt their ideas to your company style. Ask them to complete a short project designing a limited collection for one part of your company to present at second interview.

Another example could be a visual merchandiser or display assistant being given an area to dress.

Anyone who has to have any form of visual skill should be given a test as these qualities are impossible to assess by interview alone.

Manual dexterity (physical ability)

If you are recruiting someone who needs to do manual or practical work such as carpentry, machine operating, food preparation and so on, then the best way to assess this is to have the person do a trial day – see below. This is not always possible, so design a task that will test their manual dexterity that closely matches what they will be asked to do.

Psychometric and other testing

Psychometric or personality testing is designed to give an insight into the personality of the interviewee rather than their skills or experience. They can indicate if a person has the right personality traits for a specific job or company and can show, for example, if someone has the drive and ambition to be a manager but will also show if they may be too sociable and therefore may take decisions based on being liked rather than what is right for the business.

 **tip**

Psychometric tests are a useful tool when used as a small part of the recruitment process and should be introduced early enough so that candidates can have feedback and so you can use the results to target your questions in the next meeting.

Ideally your other staff will have gone through your chosen test so that you can identify what an ideal profile will be.

There are usually a battery of questions asking the candidate to express opinions or make statements about their attitude. There are no right or wrong answers and they are encouraged to answer quickly rather than analysing the options.

Psychometric tests can only be analysed by qualified consultants. This means that you have one of three options.

1 Brief the psychometric testing company on what exactly you need. They will use the brief together with your job and candidate definition to select the appropriate tests or battery of tests. They will give feedback to each candidate and present you with the report. This will give the most detailed information but will be the most costly. It is also difficult to arrange for candidates to get to another location and this will be time-consuming.

2 Someone in your organisation can be trained and then licensed to use the tests in-house, give feedback and compile the report. Cost-effectiveness will depend on how many candidates you will need to screen per year, as you will have to pay for the training and the license will be due annually. The other down side is that if your practitioner leaves the company, you will have to pay again for someone else to be trained.

3   Source a supplier who will provide the tests and then analyse them for you, usually online. This will be the most cost-effective and convenient way of conducting tests but they will be more basic than the reports in the other two options and there may not be any feedback for the candidates.

These psychometric tests are most appropriate for senior level roles or where you are looking for a specific trait across a large department where you are constantly recruiting so that the numbers involved make it more viable. If you use recruitment consultants they should also be able to advise and in some cases will conduct these for you.

Other tests can include spatial awareness, numeracy, lateral thinking, etc.

Make sure the candidates are aware that they are going to be asked to go through this procedure. Most senior people will have been through something similar before but others may not have, and you should ensure that they are comfortable with what is going to happen, how long it will take, that there are no right or wrong answers so they can't pass or fail, etc.

Trial day or afternoon

If you are recruiting for a practical job then a half-day's trial is a good way to test someone's skills. You may be hiring someone for your joinery shop who has the right qualifications and experience, but until you see them in action you cannot tell how skilled they are or at what speed they work.

If you are organising a trial, do make sure it's planned and you know what you want them to do. Let the candidate know what they are going to be doing and explain what you are looking for. This may mean that some candidates de-select themselves by deciding they are not capable of performing that task at the level you need!

brilliant tip

> The person coming for the trial day will not be on your payroll so
> make sure you have insurance cover – employers' liability, etc.

Assessment centres

If you are recruiting several candidates for the same or similar
roles, or where there is a repeated recruitment need, for example to hire trainees, you may want to consider setting up an
assessment centre.

brilliant definition

> Assessment centres can include whichever elements of the
> recruitment process you choose but typically will cover psychometric
> testing, other tests such as numeracy, a practical task, and an
> interview. They should be structured in such a way that you can put
> several candidates through the procedure at the same time.

The difficult part is setting up the first one, so decide on a
format that you can use again and again. Decide:

● which elements of the recruitment process you want to include
● who else in your company is going to be involved
● what their role will be
● how you are going to 'mark' the candidates
● at what stage candidates are going to be asked to go through
  the assessment, i.e. whether they will have a first interview.

You can use the assessment centre instead of first or second
interview stage.

The most time and cost effective way is to use it at first interview stage, and you make a decision on who to hire from there.

In some instances you may want to conduct first interviews and introduce this at second interview stage. If you are using a recruiter, remember they will do first interview so they can shortlist for your assessment centre.

Assessment centres – pros and cons

- Tests need to be planned well in advance to ensure that the relevant people are available.

- You will need to have other staff on hand to administer the tasks, etc.

- If they continue for more than two hours then you should provide refreshments.

- You need to ensure that all the people involved in the decision-making process are fully briefed on what their role is in this process and how to assess the candidates.

- The organisation and administration involved make them useful for repeat or mass recruitment needs but not for individual jobs.

- You can compare candidates when they are literally alongside each other.

Right to work

It is a legal requirement to ensure that anyone you employ has the right to work in the United Kingdom, and employing anyone who does not have this can lead to prosecution.

The United Kingdom has an ethnically diverse population and many people from ethnic minorities are British citizens, and many non-British citizens are also entitled to work here.

brilliant tip

You need to see proof of right to work but in order not to discriminate on racial grounds you must ask all of your prospective employees to provide this. Asking only those who appear not to be British may constitute unlawful discrimination.

Decide at which point in the recruitment process you are going to ask for this documentary proof, and make sure candidates are all asked to bring this with them. You must do this before they start work. Ask them to bring their passports or any other documentation that will verify their right to work in the UK. Make sure you use the same request to all the candidates.

You must see the original documents and you must check the photograph so you need to include this at one of the interview stages when you are face-to-face. It is easiest to do so at the first meeting. If you have an HR department they will advise on this and also check the documentation.

If you don't have this luxury then refer to www.ukba.homeoffice. gov.uk and study prevention of illegal working – current guidelines and codes. This will give you the up-to-date information on what documentation you need to see, together with a list of the European Economic Area members who have the right to work here and those that are members but still need other authorisation to work.

> refer to www.ukba.homeoffice.gov.uk and study prevention of illegal working

You need to see documents that show the holder is not subject to immigration control such as:

- Passport showing they are a British citizen or a citizen of the UK and Colonies having the right to abode in the UK.

- Passport or ID card from one of the members of the European Economic Area or Switzerland.

- A Residency permit, Registration Certificate or document indicating permanent residency issued by the Home Office or Border and Immigration Agency to an EEA or Swiss citizen.

- Passport or travel document endorsed to show that the holder is exempt from immigration control, is allowed to stay indefinitely in the UK, has the right to abode in the UK or has no time limit on their stay in the UK.

If your candidate cannot work in the UK then their passport will be endorsed with a stamp clearly stating that employment is prohibited or that they cannot enter or change employment, paid or unpaid, without the consent of the Secretary of State.

Verify the documents.

- Check the photograph – see the individual in person.

- Check the document dates are valid.

- If you have more than one document, do the details match? – if the names are different you will need to see documentary evidence to verify this.

- Check any stamps or visas.

- Check that they are genuine – not tampered with or altered in any way.

Take a copy of the relevant pages and keep these while the person is employed by you and for two years after they leave your employment. Relevant pages include those covering:

- Front cover of the document or the one that has the holder's personal details.

- Nationality.

- Photograph.

- Signature.
- Date of birth.
- Date of expiry.
- Biometric details (if applicable).
- UK government endorsements – i.e. giving them the right to work.

Some individuals may be granted the right to enter or remain in the UK for a limited period. You need to ensure that they can work during this time and if you hire them you will need to check their status every twelve months or until they have one of the documents listed above. Check what other documentation you need at the above website.

brilliant tip

Never assume that because an applicant has a valid National Insurance number they have the right to work. This is not the case.

References

It is good practice to take up references, although increasingly these are becoming more basic. It is a way of validating the details the candidate has given you and they are often essential in certain job categories or as a requirement for insurance policy cover.

Follow-up of references is usually in the form of written requests, as most companies will not respond to verbal enquiries, and includes asking for confirmation of the dates of employment, job role and reason for leaving.

Ensure the candidate knows that you are taking up references and who from. References from their present employer would usually be taken up once they have resigned.

Another or an additional option may be to take up a verbal trade reference from someone that the candidate knows within the industry.

 example

If you are recruiting a buyer then it may be helpful to speak to the salespeople who have sold product to them to obtain a trade reference.

Police check

If you are hiring staff to work with children or to work in an area where children will be, then you must have a police check completed. This will include people who do not regularly work under these circumstances but who have a requirement to do so, perhaps for a set period.

brilliant example

A building site manager, who is responsible for managing construction sites, in normal circumstances will not be working with or near children. However, the next site you need him to supervise is in a school.

If you are in this situation you should take professional legal advice on what you need to do and when you should include it in your selection process.

Medical

A pre-employment medical may be company policy, a pre-requisite for private health insurance cover, or the candidate's role may involve operating machinery, driving, flying, etc.

Medicals are expensive and time-consuming, so confine these, if possible, to your final shortlisted candidates.

Offer

The final part of your process will be the offer. Make sure you know what the successful candidate is currently earning, including their full package, so that your offer is going to be interesting to them – see Chapter 15, The Offer.

 **summary**

- Include enough elements to ensure you have sufficient information about your candidate to enable you to make a valid judgement.
- Make certain that everyone involved understands the job role and the candidate requirements.
- Develop a marking structure that everyone in the process can use.
- Ensure that you are being fair and putting each through the same process and giving them identical information.
- If you use a practical task make sure the candidates are fully briefed on what to expect and what you are looking for.
- Decide if psychometric or other testing is appropriate for your situation.

PART 2

The interviews

CHAPTER 5

Be prepared

Aims and question types

There is no mystique to interviewing. We use the process every day in a variety of situations, as it is an exchange of information between two parties which you then have to analyse.

However, if you are new to interviewing, do not interview frequently or have little or no training in interview skills, it can be nerve-racking and fraught with pitfalls. Remember that however unsure or nervous you may feel, the candidate will be feeling even less confident.

> however unsure or nervous you may feel, the candidate will be feeling even less confident

The key to a successful interview is in the planning. Unplanned interviews or under-prepared interviewers can turn an interview into a chat – a pleasant but unproductive interlude which will result in your hiring the candidate you like best but not necessarily the most suitable one!

brilliant tip

By planning your interview you will avoid having a situation where the interviewee answers your question with a very short or even one-word answer, leaving you struggling to think of what to ask next.

The interview plan

Try planning your interview around the following:

- Review the job and candidate specification and the candidate's CV.

- Make sure you note any points you are not sure about in their details – job titles you are not familiar with, points they have made that you do not understand.

- Decide what questions to ask to cover these.

- Highlight any gaps in their work history to ensure you learn the reasons behind these.

- Make a note of any shortfalls in the CV, i.e. skills that you need to have but are not obvious from the candidate's details.

- Decide what questions to ask to cover these areas.

- Put together a series of other relevant questions to ensure that you have enough information to compare the candidates and decide which to take to the next stage.

- Base these questions on the needs that you have identified in the candidate specification.

- Review your questions to ensure they are not discriminatory in any way.

It is illegal to ask any questions that may be discriminatory. Grounds of discrimination include sex, race, disability, sexual orientation, religion or belief and age: see Chapter 16, Discrimination.

 **tip**

Take a copy of the CV so that you can highlight points that need further clarification, leaving a clean one for anyone else involved in the next stage of the selection process.

Interview timing

Once you have planned your questions, think about the timings for your interview schedule. Decide how long you are going to allocate for each interview by calculating how much time is needed for each section.

● How long do you need to obtain the right level of information from the candidate for this stage of the recruitment process?

● The interview is a two-way process as you are not the only one making a decision, so allow time to give the interviewee enough information about the company and the job to enable them to make an informed choice.

● Allow time for the candidate's questions.

● Include a break between interviews to write up your notes.

If you happen to have shortlisted more than one candidate from the same company, try to avoid having their interviews running consecutively so that you can maintain confidentiality.

Timing an interview can be difficult, especially for the inexperienced. You need to control the interview so that you keep to your schedule. If you have an overly chatty candidate who wants to give you more information than you need, try using more 'closed' questions than you would normally. This will help you to interrupt their flow but will make sure that you get the facts that you need. ('Closed' questions are explained later in this chapter.) You can also try using body language such as folding your arms which will indicate that you are closed to further conversation. At the end of the interview these talkative candidates will usually want the last word and you may actually have to stand up and show them the door!

The opposite is the quiet candidate. They can also be helped along by body language. Try leaning back in your chair with your arms open or at your side to indicate that you are relaxed.

When they do start to open up, look interested, lean forward again as if you are deeply engrossed in what they are saying, nod to acknowledge that you understand.

 **tip**

Keep a close eye on time as it is very easy to run over if you have a good candidate or a very chatty one. Sit so that you can easily see a clock – it's less obvious than looking at your watch.

Starting your interview

Interviews are often conducted under pressure when time is short and it is easy to miss some basic details, so don't forget the following:

- Make sure the candidates know how to get to the interview. This may sound obvious, but you go to your building every day. They don't!

- Make sure they know where to report to and who to ask for.

- To get the best from your applicant make them as comfortable and as much at ease as possible; this is an interview, not an interrogation. Simple things like making sure they are not sitting in direct sunlight or next to a noisy office will make a difference.

- Welcome the interviewee to the company and thank them for coming to see you.

- Introduce yourself and give your job title, and if it is not obvious explain what you do and whether the job you are recruiting for will report to you.

- Explain the recruitment process – second interview, tests, etc., with a timeline.

- Explain what will happen today and the timeline on feedback, i.e. 'Today I want to find out more about you and tell you about our company. We have shortlisted ten people, and you are the third and we hope to have decided on second interviews by early next week.'

- Give them a brief introduction to the company and the role you are recruiting for (you can go into more detail at the end of the interview if appropriate).

- Take notes. If you do not interview regularly you will not remember the interviewee unless you take notes.

brilliant tip

Use the candidate's name frequently during your meeting to help build up rapport and personalise the interview.

Aim of the interviews

The aim of the first interview is to get an overall impression of the candidate and have enough information to compare them to others, but you don't need to cover every point in this first meeting. Concentrate on their experience, including any gaps on their CV, reasons for leaving and any points you need more information on.

You must also give the candidate some information on your company and the job, ideally including a copy of the job and candidate specification: this may have been sent to them prior to interview. Answer any questions they have, and 'sell' them the role. It's their decision too!

Unless you are recruiting a junior level role you will need to conduct a second and, possibly, further interviews and these can concentrate on more in-depth questions to discover if the candidate has the skills you need.

However, there is a danger that this and subsequent meetings can become a repeat of the first one with many of the same questions being asked, so you need to decide on your reasons for the next interview and what you want to gain out of it.

As we saw in Chapter 4, Your Recruitment and Selection Process, the reasons for further interviews will include some or all of the following:

● You need to ask more in-depth questions that you did not cover in the first interview. The questions at second interview should be planned to match the skills you have identified on your candidate or person specification and cover areas that you did not cover in the first meeting.

● The candidates need to meet other people in your organisation. If other people are now involved or you are the line manager now stepping into the process, make sure everyone understands what was covered at first interview. You may want the candidate to re-cap but you do not need to go into detail about their work again.

● There is a practical task or some form of testing for them to complete.

● The candidates, even junior ones, need to have a sense of achievement if you offer them the job.

● You simply cannot decide between two or more candidates. Plan a second interview that will give you some more information to help you decide.

every question you ask at interview should be targeted at getting specific information

The overall aim of the interviews is to find the right candidate, so review each interview stage to make sure you are achieving this.

How to ask the right type of questions

Every question you ask at interview should have a purpose and should be targeted at getting specific information.

 brilliant definition

> There are two types of question which can both be used to good effect. The main one you want to use will be 'open' questions that generate information, and the others are 'closed' questions that can be used to clarify a point.

Closed questions starting with 'Did...', 'Do...', 'Is...', 'Was...', etc. will generate 'Yes' or 'No' answers. These should be avoided when you are gathering information, as you want to generate more detailed answers. A short answer to a closed question can leave you struggling to think what to ask next. So you will always start your questioning with open type questions.

However, closed questions can be used effectively to clarify points, especially if you are trying to get a conclusion to a question.

Q Why did you leave your last company? (Open question to generate information.)

A I wasn't really getting on.

Q Why was that? (Open question to draw more information.)

A I don't really know.

Q Did something specific happen to make you leave? (Closed question to clarify the above.)

A I had an argument with my boss and decided it was better to leave.

Q Did you leave of your own accord? (Closed question to get final closure on the point.)

During the interview use open questions, except in situations like the one above, where you cannot be given one-word or very short answers.

Open questions starting with 'Who...', 'What...', 'Where...', 'When...', 'How...' will draw more detailed information from your interviewee and they will also give you time to think about your next question.

They should still be targeted to get the information you want and not used as general openings.

brilliant tip

Never use very general open questions like 'Tell me about yourself?' This will confuse an already nervous candidate who will not know where to start and will not know what information you want from them.

Another interview favourite is 'Talk me through your CV.' That may not turn out to be too onerous if you are interviewing a younger candidate but you are leaving yourself open to them starting at the beginning of their career or even their life!

Do not take answers at face value. Check their answers by asking them to expand on their answer and give examples. This is usually known as a competence-based interview and can be used for all levels of applicants.

Asking for examples can also help you to understand a comment that the candidate makes that may relate directly to their company and doesn't make sense taken out of context. Questions can include openings such as 'Give me an example', 'Describe a situation', 'How did you deal with', and so on.

As well as asking for their examples, try to include scenarios that the candidates may face in your organisation and ask how they would respond.

Avoiding obvious questions

When you start to probe into skills you will need to ask more in-depth questions but try to avoid the obvious interview questions such as 'What do you think are your strengths and weaknesses?' Candidates will have rehearsed answers for such questions and will devise answers they think you want to hear. If you want to identify these areas but want a less contrived answer, try asking these questions:

Q What part of your job do you enjoy most?

Q What are you best at?

Q What are you not so good at?

Q How can that be improved?

brilliant summary

- Identify what the aim of the interview is.
- Put together your interview plan.
- Use mainly open questions.
- Avoid the obvious questions that can have rehearsed answers.
- Ask for examples to back up their answers, or set scenarios for them to comment on.
- Make sure you give the candidate enough information to make their decision.

CHAPTER 6

Experience

Present and past work history

The easiest place to start your questions is with their present or most recent job, and work backwards. Never start with their first job, as this could be some years ago and may not even be relevant. Depending on the work history you may not need to go through every job. Build your understanding of what they do by finding out about

> the easiest place to start your questions is with their present or most recent job

their company first, then their level of seniority and how they are managed, before moving on to specifics of their role. This will enable you to put their experience in context and understand it more clearly.

Questions about present and previous companies

To get the interview started ask the following type of question about their present or most recent employer:

Q I don't know your company that well / at all so can you tell me what they do?

Q Who are their main customers?

Q What is their turnover?

Q How many staff are there?

(Q) Who are their main competitors?

(Q) What other services do they provide?

All of these questions will help you understand the company and will also give you an insight into how involved the candidate is. In junior roles they may not know some of the answers and this may not be important, but as roles increase in seniority then you will expect them to have this information to hand. Some people work in isolation and do not have a natural curiosity to find things out. This may work well in some companies but in others people need to be naturally curious and therefore have an overall understanding of the company and how their role fits within it.

(Q) What is the company culture like?

(Q) Do you enjoy that type of environment?

(Q) Which other type of environments have you worked in and which did you prefer?

These questions will help you establish if this candidate is likely to fit into your company culture.

brilliant tip

Interviews are primarily to help you select a candidate but they can have other advantages. Use your interviews as a way of finding out what other companies are doing, especially if they are competitors. It may inspire you to look at a different way of working in your business or other potential customers you could approach. Keep a note of any senior managers that your interviewee mentions as you may want to headhunt them in the future.

Questions establishing level of seniority

Now you have an understanding of their company you will be better equipped to understand their role. You now need to quantify it and find out where they sit in the organisation. Some people have very grand titles but are still several rungs away from the main decision makers.

Q Who do you report to?

This question on its own will tell you what job title their boss has, but without the next two questions it may be meaningless as you will not know how many other layers of management there are above them.

Q Who does your manager report to?

You may want to follow this with:

Q And who do they report to?

or even ask:

Q Can you give me an overview of the company structure so that I have a full understanding of what level you are at?

If your candidate reports to, for example, a General Manager, it is easy to assume that there is only one General Manager who oversees the running of the whole company and reports to the directors, but in some companies this can be the title for a head of department, of which there are many. Check where they are in the company.

Q How many people report to your manager?

This should indicate how much independence his or her team members have.

brilliant tip

If the candidate refers by name to their manager, or whoever they are discussing, then use it when asking them questions rather than referring to 'your manager', to help personalise the interview.

Q Does anyone report to you directly / indirectly?

It is worth asking about indirect reports as some of these relationships can be the most difficult to manage. Also some businesses work on a matrix system where there are very few direct reports but many indirect ones.

Q How many are there in your team?

The size of their team, either direct reports or fellow team members, gives you an idea of the scope of the group they are in.

Q What do the rest of your team members do?

Again this can apply to direct reports in their team or the other team members, and will help identify how key their role is within the business.

Q How many other people do the same job as you?

If you are one of 50 clerks in a general admin office you will have little chance to show initiative, influence decisions and so on. Whereas, if you are the only clerk in a small company working for various managers this could be very different.

These questions will help you get a measure of their actual level of seniority – are they just one of many doing a role or are they the only one fulfilling an important function?

If you are interviewing for a man-management role you will need to ask more questions about their management experience and style. At this stage you are going through the basics and these areas will be covered later in the interview.

Questions to establish how they are managed

Q How is your work overseen or checked?

Some work can be easily checked and monitored but in other cases it may be very difficult to do and the employee may be able to continue doing a poor job without it being detected. Consider how their answer may or may not enable them to thrive in your environment.

Q Do you enjoy working in that way?

Just because they work in a particular environment doesn't mean they like it or want to stay in it, so check out their thoughts. Most people like to be monitored in some way so that they know they are doing a good job, but not everyone relishes being pressurised for results. There is not a right or wrong answer to these types of questions as people are just different and you need to be able to assess if this particular person will work well in your set-up.

Q How is your work generated?

To help you decide if they will 'fit' your company you may need to know if they are given work or if they have to generate it themselves.

Q How often do you meet with your manager?

Q What format does this take? Is this formal or informal?

Q Are you expected to produce written reports?

Q How do you resolve problems? What issues would you refer to your manager?

If a candidate is already used to working in a similar environment to yours then their initial learning curve will be less than someone from a different type of company.

Some of these questions are aimed at more junior candidates, but remember that even Managing Directors are accountable and therefore 'managed' by someone so you will need to change some of the wording or re-phrase the questions. For example:

Q What dictates how you plan your time?

Q How often do you report into your chairman?

Questions about specific duties and responsibilities

You should now understand the company set-up and where the interviewee's role fits. Now you need to find out which are the important elements of their job and whether this will match your requirements, so try asking:

Q Can you talk me through a typical day / week / month?

This will help you get an understanding of their job even if it is one you have never come across before.

Q So what percentage of your time do you spend on each task?

This determines which part of their job they have the most experience in. CVs can be misleading and can read as if the main focus of a job is one thing when in fact they only spend five minutes a day doing it. The answer will also help you establish the main part of the job and will help determine if it is the level of experience you need.

Q How do you deal with a particular task?

There may be a specific area that you also need covered and it will be important to establish how they are used to dealing with it.

Q Which of your tasks takes priority?

This will help assess how much experience they have in a given task.

brilliant tip

Never assume, even if you have previously done the same job or worked in the same company as a candidate you are interviewing, that you don't need to ask as many or even any questions about it. The company WILL have changed since you left and the roles certainly will. By assuming you know something you can miss a key part of the candidate's skills or assume they will have fulfilled certain functions which they have not covered.

Q Who allocates your time?

Shows whether they work unsupervised and plan their own day, or work to a more closely monitored regime.

Q Which other departments do you liaise with?

Liaison may not be part of their job at all but you may need it in your company.

Q How do you communicate with other departments?

Identifies what communication skills they have to utilise.

Q Which do you prefer?

People generally prefer doing things they are good at so this question should give you an indication of where their strengths lie.

Q How do you communicate with other groups, for example customers?

This is another question to elaborate on their communication skills.

If they have not mentioned during this discourse something that you thought they would have done or something you were hoping they had covered, then ask them specifically about this.

Q Part of our role involves being the first point of contact for complaints. Who deals with this in your company?

This may well prove to be the biggest part of this person's role, and so obvious to them that they didn't mention it. If you are not sure, always ask: otherwise you could discount a really good candidate simply because you didn't know.

🡥 brilliant summary

- Work through their CV, starting with the most recent or present role.
- Concentrate on the jobs most relevant to the experience you need.
- Get a good understanding of their present and past companies.
- Find out where they 'sit' within the organisation.
- Get to grips with their duties and responsibilities.
- Identify how the majority of their time is spent.

CHAPTER 7

Problem areas

Gaps on CVs and reasons for leaving

Problem areas mainly occur when you start probing into gaps on CVs or reasons for leaving. You need to make sure you have all the details to decide whether these situations are a problem for you and your company.

Questions regarding 'gaps' and anomalies on CVs

You should highlight any gaps on the CV and look out for any unusual patterns, such as always having a gap between jobs even if they are short periods, dates that don't tally or information that you know isn't correct. These are likely to be simple mistakes or easily explained, but don't ignore them; they could indicate negative issues and need further investigation.

> highlight any gaps on the CV and look out for any unusual patterns

Ⓠ I notice that you appear to have been out of work for nine months before your present job. Why was that?

Ⓠ I notice there was a year between leaving university and starting your first job. What were you doing?

There may be valid reasons for these gaps but these questions could highlight problems such as medical issues. If this is the case, investigate further.

Q What was the problem?

Q Is it resolved now / how is it affecting you?

Q Does it affect your work?

Often gaps are where women have taken time out to have children, and therefore can cover several years, and you may want to ensure they are now ready to come back to work.

Q What has made you apply for jobs now?

Q Have you kept up-to-date with legislation / systems / research / the market, etc., during the last few years?

Q How have you done this / how do you intend to get up to speed?

brilliant tip

You can ask questions concerning ability to do the job, but do not ask questions concerning child care arrangements as these could be discriminatory. You will have to assume that these have been taken care of.

We will look at issues like the above and related topics in Chapter 8, Education.

Questions on reasons for leaving

You also need to ask the reason for leaving each job. They are always a good insight into the candidate and you need to understand their reasons for leaving to ensure there aren't any problems in their present job as well as in past ones. It will also help you to decide what motivates them and to assess if you can offer that motivation.

Q So why did you leave that company / why are you looking to leave your present company?

The answer to this may be very straightforward such as, 'my partner had to relocate for their job so I had to move too', but most answers to this question will consist of variations on 'more money', 'promotion', or 'a better job'. Very few people leave a company purely for more money. Their reasons will be more complex and may include money, but are likely to be more about self-esteem generally. Don't take the answer at face value. They all need further investigation so ask more questions about it.

Q I understand your partner was re-locating but your company also has offices locally, so couldn't you have transferred?

If someone is doing well the obvious thing will be for them to see if they can relocate with the same company. It may not have been possible but they may have been turned down or may not have asked, so you need to know why.

Q Why didn't you ask for a transfer?

They may have genuine reasons they didn't ask to transfer, such as a real desire to change job / company, time off to sort out the re-location, the offices may have been in the same town but too far to commute, or they may have been under-performing or not enjoying their role. You need to know which, so keep asking until you are clear about the reasons behind this.

Q Why couldn't they offer you a transfer?

Q Why didn't you accept the transfer you were offered?

If their reason for leaving is for more money, try asking the following:

Q Was there no way of earning more money where you were?

The usual way of earning more money is to work longer hours or get promoted. Neither of these may have been options, but make sure you know.

Ⓠ How much of an increase did you get in the next job?

If they claim to have left for more money but in actual fact the increase they got was negligible, then there were clearly other reasons (remember, however, that the increase may not have been just on basic salary so ask them to talk you through the package). Try to draw out the other reasons by giving them ample opportunity to put them forward.

Ⓠ Were there any other reasons for leaving?

Promotion is another answer that is proffered at interview.

Ⓠ What were the promotional prospects where you were?

There may have been none at all – it was / is a small company and people rarely leave. If this is the only reason they left or are thinking of leaving then it will indicate ambition and drive, so make sure you can provide for it. If you are getting these answers from someone who has been in the company for a number of years without promotion then it's likely there is another reason they have chosen to leave now.

Ⓠ Why have you decided you want promotion now?

Keep pushing until you are satisfied with the answer.

brilliant tip

Also be wary of those who have a track record of moving every two years or less. In some sectors or roles this may be quite usual but in others it can indicate a low boredom threshold, an inability to commit for any length of time or that they are very ambitious.

The ambitious ones will be able to give very definite reasons for moving and should be able to demonstrate their climb up the ladder but the others will be vague and the career progression less obvious. Decide which of these you want.

(Q) Did you apply for promotion – what happened?

(Q) So, if you didn't get the promotion, who did, and why do you think they got it instead of you?

(Q) Was this fair? Why not?

With these questions you are trying to establish if this person has not been considered suitable for promotion and why. Just because they were turned down doesn't mean they aren't right for your job, but you need to assess this.

Questions on redundancy

A genuine redundancy is because the company was down-sizing, a particular role or group of roles was deemed unnecessary, re-structuring left a level of roles redundant or the company closed completely. There are very set procedures for making someone redundant, although many companies even now do not always follow these, but to make sure this was a genuine case ask the following:

(Q) Did you volunteer for redundancy? Why?

(Q) Why were you made redundant?

(Q) How many others were made redundant at that same time?

(Q) How did they choose who would be made redundant?

(Q) Were you offered any alternative jobs?

(Q) How were they going to cover your workload?

These questions will help you determine if this was a genuine redundancy or just a way of getting them out of the business.

> ### ✹ brilliant tip
>
> It is not unusual to see candidates being made redundant and then only in their next job for a short period, or even being made redundant a second time. Redundancy has a major psychological impact on most people and many panic, especially after a stable track record, and take their next job without always giving it the careful consideration they would normally. Most will accept they made a mistake and if the rest of their background is stable then this really is a 'blip'.

Questions on dismissal

Very few people will put the word 'dismissal' on their CV and when you ask about reasons for leaving they will often try to avoid it, possibly without actually lying. It can be an emotive subject, and remember some dismissals aren't fair. If you think someone is not being open about a reason for leaving, ask:

> very few people will put the word 'dismissal' on their CV

Ⓠ So, what would your ex-manager or the HR department say if I wrote or rang them for a reference?

This should draw out the truth, and you can then give them time to explain further.

Ⓠ So, what actually happened?

Ⓠ Was that fair?

Ⓠ Have you appealed against it?

If we feel that we have been unfairly dismissed most of us will take it further and not just walk away.

Closed questions, where a simple Yes or No is the only answer, can be used to good effect in these situations. If you feel the candidate is still not being entirely truthful use direct, closed questions such as:

Q So, you were dismissed?

Q So you were allowed to resign rather than being dismissed?

Q So it was a personality clash with your boss?

brilliant summary

- Make sure you check any gaps in the CV.
- Identify any unusual patterns and check them out.
- Find out the reasons for leaving each job.
- Do not take these answers at face value – ask for more clarification.
- Use 'closed' questions to get straight answers to difficult facts.

CHAPTER 8

Education

Training and questions for school and college leavers

For some roles it will have been identified that you need a certain level of education, a specific qualification or training or you may be interviewing a school or college leaver, so questions need to be targeted around this.

Questions on education

Questions on education may be irrelevant for more experienced candidates unless they have been a mature student, there is a specific area you need to cover or you have highlighted an anomaly on their CV.

Q I notice that you got three very good 'A' Levels but you didn't go to university. Why was that?

Q I notice that you got very good GCSE results but you are not going on to further study. Why is that?

brilliant tip

If this is a candidate who has just completed their 'A' Levels or GCSE or similar, you need to make sure they are not just looking for a gap-year role or something to do while they decide what to do next.

Push them a bit further by asking:

Q Would you like to go on to university or college in the future?

look for any irregularities on the CV such as taking four years to do a three-year course

Look for any irregularities on the CV such as taking four years to do a three-year course, dropping out before completing the course, changing courses. There may be very valid reasons, but they need to be verified.

Q The course you did is usually a three-year one but you took four years to complete it. Why was that?

Taking longer to complete a course can often highlight problems. There may have been a trauma in the family or a medical problem.

- What was it?
- Has it been dealt with?
- If it was a medical problem, have they recovered or is it ongoing?
- How will this affect them? Are they still having treatment?

Q I notice that you did two years of your degree but didn't complete it. Why was that?

This may also highlight a problem, as above, or it can indicate an inability to commit and see something through.

Q You changed course in year two. Why was that?

Changing course in year one happens a lot as students quite simply make the wrong decision on the course, but getting as far as year two and then deciding to change may also indicate an inability to see things through.

Q You did a degree in criminology but you are now applying for our role as a sales executive. Why is that?

If your candidate has studied a vocational degree, i.e. one that leads directly to a specific job and career path, but is now applying to you for a completely different type of role you need to ensure that they are not just filling in while waiting for something in their chosen field.

Q What did you gain from the course?

Q In hindsight would you have chosen a different one?

The above will help to clarify their reasons for opting to change direction now.

Many courses include work placements and these are useful ways to establish the candidate's work ethics.

Q Tell me about the work placement you did as part of your course?

Q How did you get it?

Q What did you learn from it?

Q Do you think it was relevant to the course?

Q Do you think it is relevant to this job?

If you are recruiting for a specialist of some sort just having the initial qualification may not be enough for your current role so you need to establish how they keep up to speed.

Q You qualified some time ago. How do you keep up-to-date?

Q Do you have a system for this?

You may want to ask specific questions relating to your role, such as:

Q What do you think of the new legislation on . . . ?

Q How would you use the new research on . . . ?

Q Are you familiar with the new procedures on . . . ?

Questions on training

Some employees learn on the job but it is useful to know what training, in-house or external, they have had, especially if this will enhance the skills you require.

(Q) What training courses have you been on?

(Q) Were they in-house or external?

A lot of in-house sessions may only be applicable to that company and consist of systems training, etc. so find out what they were and who took them in order to evaluate the relevance.

(Q) What did you think of them?

(Q) Who conducted them?

(Q) How were you selected to go on the course?

brilliant tip

Some candidates may have asked to go on the course or even sourced the course as it was an area they needed assistance in. This shows a willingness to learn and initiative, and clearly indicates that they were well thought-of for the company to organise this for them.

Additional questions for school and college leavers

Some interviewers find these candidates the most difficult to interview, and worry about what to ask as there is no work history to go on.

Use the questions on education and then look for any work experience or temporary jobs and use the work-related questions for these. With so many people now going to university you will need to look at these areas to differentiate between young graduates.

Another area to discuss may be voluntary or charity work especially with so many students taking gap years.

Q Have you done any voluntary work or charity work, and if so what?

Q How did you get involved?

Q How long was it for?

Q What were your duties?

Q What did you gain from it?

Q What was the biggest challenge you faced while doing this?

Try looking at positions they have held at school / college or in clubs, etc.

If they were a prefect / head girl or boy / club captain:

Q How were you chosen?

Q What were your duties?

Q Did you have to organise anything?

Q Did you enjoy it?

Q What was the most difficult thing about holding this position?

Look at hobbies and interests as they will tell you whether they have drive to get on with things; they may show commitment especially if they have completed one of the Duke of Edinburgh schemes.

If the candidates enjoys/has done . . .

Q What does it involve?

Q What do you like about it?

Q How did you get involved?

Q Are your friends involved?

Q How often do you do it / attend?

Their hobbies may be more passive, such as reading or going to the cinema.

Ⓠ What type of books / films do you enjoy most?

Ⓠ What was the last book you read / film you saw?

Ⓠ What did you think of it?

Ⓠ What are you currently reading / planning to see?

With hobbies and interests look for the candidates that have found interests of their own rather than getting involved because their parents think it's a good idea. Have they shown commitment to their chosen hobbies or are they more passing phases? Have they put hobbies in just to fill the page and cannot remember the last film they saw?

Finally find out why they want to work for you and check their understanding of what they are applying for.

Ⓠ What do you know about this company?

Ⓠ Why are you applying to this company?

Ⓠ What do you think the job involves?

Ⓠ Why will you be good at this job?

Ⓠ What else are you considering?

↗ brilliant summary

- Cover education if you have a specific requirement or you are interviewing school or college leavers.
- Look for any anomalies and establish why they have occurred.
- Make sure your company is not being used as a fill-in.
- Find out what internal and external training they have done.
- School leavers – what do they know about your company / job?
- School leavers – find out what experience they have – voluntary work, hobbies, etc.

CHAPTER 9

Establishing the candidate's skills

Matching them to your requirements

Below are skills that you may have identified on your candidate profile and want to ask further questions on. Although it is not a definitive list it will help compile the type of questions you need for other categories. Remember to focus your questions on the skills that you have identified as essential.

> focus your questions on the skills that you have identified as essential

Questions relating to organisational ability

Q How do you organise your day / department / team?

You can use one or all of the above depending on the level of candidate. For junior roles you will only want to know that they are capable of organising their daily routine, but senior people will have other organisational challenges. It is easy for people to say they are organised but you need evidence of this, so try and find examples of where they have to use their organisational abilities.

Q Is how you plan your day / department / team your own decision?

Find out if this is actually their skills being put to use or whether they are following someone else's guidelines.

Q What factors do you have to take into consideration?

Sometimes organising is a simple task because there are few considerations. If there are many items or other people to consider then it becomes more complex and a greater test of organisational skills.

Q Give me an example of something else you have organised.

If you are interviewing someone who has worked in a role where the main focus is organisational, such as events management or conference organiser, or you are recruiting for this type of role, you will want to ask for several examples and go into this in more depth. Otherwise use this question to build on the information you have, and help establish what level of skill they have.

Q Did you organise this from start to finish or just part of it?

Make sure that when you are told that they organised something it was the complete task and not just an insignificant part of it.

Q What difficulties did you encounter?

This will help identify the depth of their involvement and their ability to problem solve.

Q How did you overcome them?

 **tip**

To be a good organiser you often need to be able to problem solve. There is no right or wrong answer here but you are looking for the fact that they recognised problems and overcame them.

Questions to assess communication skills

Communication is key in so many roles and you will have considered what type of skills you need and who the communication is with. These questions will help you understand what communication channels the candidate is familiar with and which they excel in.

(Q) Who do you have to communicate with on a daily / weekly / monthly basis?

(Q) How do you communicate upwards, that is to your manager, for example? How do you communicate downwards to the people that report to you directly? And to other teams?

The way you communicate can depend on who you are communicating with, and often different approaches are better for different people and situations.

(Q) Which method of communication do you prefer?

You are looking for a reply that mirrors the needs of your business. People usually excel in areas that they enjoy.

(Q) How would you improve the communication in your company?

Strong communicators will be frustrated by systems that they perceive do not get the point across. Here you want valid ideas, not complaints.

(Q) Have you ever initiated any improvements, and what were they?

Someone who can understand the problems and offer workable solutions will be a valued member of staff. Others may just want to interfere and change things for the sake of it. Try differentiating by asking the next two questions.

(Q) Did your improvements work?

They may have suggested changes, but were they well thought out and did they improve the system?

(Q) What was the feedback from other staff?

People do not like change but if they see it as an improvement they will come round.

Questions on management style

The next set of questions is for team leaders upwards and will help you appraise their management style and skills as well as their decision-making ability and judgement. The questions will aid you in your evaluation of their skills against the ones that you need.

Q How would you describe your management style?

You can expect a routine answer to this such as 'firm but fair', but it is the lead-in to further questions.

Q Can you demonstrate that with an example?

Make them back up this answer, and ask them for more examples until you can appraise what their style is.

Q How would your boss describe your management style?

Q Why would he / she describe it that way?

Q Can you give me an example of why they would think that?

Q What do you think about that?

Q How would your team describe your management style? Can you give me an example of why they would think that?

Q Has your style ever been criticised / praised? If so, by whom? Was this fair? How did you respond?

Using the questions above will draw out more information on how they manage. Are they aware of what others think, have they adapted their style, taken on constructive criticism, or carried on regardless? Is this the type of style that works well in your company?

Q Management techniques are also used to manage upwards. How do you manage your manager and his / her expectations? Can you give me an example?

A good manager not only manages their team but often has to manage upwards and convince their manager of something that will be right for their team, or manage expectations which are not going to be in line with predictions.

Q How is your team structured? Did you structure it?

You may be looking for someone who has put a team together or re-structured an existing one.

Q Have you ever re-structured a team? Why? Did it work?

They will need to be able to put together an efficient team structured in a logical way so that the team members are clear on what their team role is. They should be able to show that there was a good reason to re-structure and not just a whim.

Q What problems have you had in the team? How did you resolve them?

Managing often involves dealing with internal conflict and disagreements. It's part of human nature and a good manager needs to be able to handle these situations. You may want to ask for more examples here to cover different types of problem, and you can give a scenario and ask how they would deal with it.

> managing often involves dealing with internal conflict and a good manager needs to be able to handle these situations

► brilliant example

You had someone in the finance team doing a good job, with great analytical skills, but part of their role involved written reports which they couldn't compile competently. The rest of their peer group were constantly having to assist and were getting fed up with it. What would you do?

You want to hear a solution that demonstrates that they can analyse the problem and resolve it. Remember they don't know how your company operates so their solution may not work in your company. They should also pick up on the fact that the finance clerk is doing a good job, so moving them to a different department or dismissing them because they can't complete this one part of their job are not useful suggestions. Hopefully they will identify this as a training need and propose some form of training or mentoring to help.

Questions on decision-making ability

Good decisions are based on an understanding of the situation with all the facts to hand, and an ability to work out the best solution and then be able to act on it. We all learn from our mistakes so decision makers will improve if they review their decisions and consider how they could have responded differently.

(Q) **What decisions do you have to make on a regular basis?**

Many people have to take decisions but you need to know at what level they are taking them. Do their regular decisions include what time everyone goes to lunch, or is it their decision to decide whether to launch a new product at a cost of millions of pounds?

(Q) **What other decisions do you get involved in?**

(Q) **Which is the most far-reaching decision you have taken?**

(Q) **What was the outcome of this?**

(Q) **Can you talk me through the thought process you went through to make that decision?**

This will give you the parameters of their influence and level of their decision making.

(Q) **Does anyone else get involved in any of your decisions? Can you describe a scene where this decision would be taken?**

Very few companies can accommodate autocrats so it is important to understand how prospective employees reach their decision. Again there is no right or wrong answer, but is this someone who simply reacts on their first instinct without any consultation with others or stopping to consider the situation further? Such a person may not be what you are looking for.

Q Do you get advice on any decisions? In what form, and from whom?

Q If others are involved, who actually has the final decision?

brilliant example

You would expect advice to be sought from the experts such as Human Resources in the case of a disciplinary situation. It may be important to discover whether the candidate seeks advice and then makes the decision based on it, or whether the situation is then handed over to the expert.

Q What was the most difficult decision you have had to make, and why?

This may not necessarily have had a big impact on the company, but you are looking for someone who will take and see through difficult decisions.

Q Were you happy with that decision, or in hindsight could you have chosen a different one?

If it was their most difficult decision you will expect them to have a view of it, and with more experience they might have handled it differently.

Q What has been the most successful decision you have made?

This could have been a more personal decision like changing jobs or setting up their own business. Look at the thoughts behind this – were they logical, practical, and sensible?

(Q) Could it have been more successful? In what way?

Did they miss a crucial fact that could have had implications for their decision?

(Q) What was the worst decision you have made, and what impact did it have? What decision should you have taken? How did you rectify the situation?

No one is infallible, but did they get themselves out of the problem they had created and have they learned from their mistake?

Questions on financial skills

You need to find out the scope of their financial decision-making. Is it confined to their department or is it wider? Financially do they look after the stationery budget or are they involved in company financial strategy?

(Q) Does your role include financial decisions? At what level?

(Q) Do you set any budgets? What are they?

Most managers will work to budgets but these may have been set by others and they have had little or no input into them. Establish here how much involvement they have had.

(Q) What is the process?

(Q) Who else is involved?

If they put together or are involved in the budget process, discover how this works and decide if this experience will give them the skills to match your budgeting skills.

(Q) How would you change the process if you could?

Budgets are always a knotty subject and it is difficult to find a process that everyone considers fair. The answer needs to show logic and understanding of why the system is in place.

Q Have you worked through your own budgets, and how many times?

They may have set budgets but not had long enough to see them through the year or longer, so there is no way of assessing their success.

Q How successful were they? Did your department / company come in on budget?

Budgets are a financial planning tool so a successful one is an accurate one. Some candidates may see setting a budget and then coming in well below it as a success, but if it had been accurate then additional money could have been used elsewhere.

Questions on sales skills and ability

Given the outgoing nature of salespeople they can be the most difficult to assess, and asking for examples and further explanations here is vital.

Q How is your sales performance measured?

To understand how well they are doing you will need to know their key performance indicators. As discussed in Chapter 1, Identifying the Needs of the Business, they may be measured purely on their sales but this can include turnover, profitability, opening of new accounts, etc., etc. If their measurement of success is different from yours, ask them specifically how many new accounts they have opened this season / year.

Q How well are you doing against your current / previous target?

Now you need to discover if they are hitting target, and if not, ask why.

Q What has been your biggest percentage increase, and how did you achieve that?

This maybe due to their diligence but there are likely to be other factors, so probe into it.

(Q) Were there any other factors?

This increase could have coincided with a major advertising campaign, or one of their retail customers opened ten new shops that season, and so on. Identify how much of this was down to their own skill and hard work and how much was due to other influences.

(Q) Was anyone else involved?

Their manager may have been doing a lot of the visits with them so that they could take over a new type of account, in which case who did do the sales?

(Q) Who sets the strategy for targeting new accounts?

Understanding the market may be a big part of your sales team job. Does this candidate know it, or is someone else passing on the leads and they follow them up?

(Q) How do you set the strategy?

You may want someone who simply bangs on doors, or you may need a more sophisticated strategic approach.

(Q) What criteria do you use?

You may not be worried about brand identity so the criteria on who you sell to may be very open, but what about credit ratings, etc? If you are more brand-aware then you want to ensure this candidate understands what will be important in assessing new accounts.

(Q) Where do you get the information from for the criteria?

How resourceful are they or how dependent on having information fed to them?

Q **What strategy do you use to maintain and increase sales to existing accounts?**

If there is pressure to open new accounts, sometimes existing ones can get ignored. How do they ensure this doesn't happen and how do they increase sales with these customers?

Q **What do you do at a sales presentation?**

The answer to this will vary enormously depending on the market and the type of product. What sort of presentations will they need to do in your organisation, have they done these or are they capable of doing them? You may have decided to include a sales presentation in your selection process to check this out – see Chapter 4, Your Recruitment and Selection Process.

Q **How often do you speak to /see your customers?**

This again will vary but find out if they have the same approach that you are looking for.

Q **What would your customers say about you?**

brilliant tip

A trade reference can prove very interesting. Do they buy from this person because they just have to stock the product, or do they buy their product, which is similar to many others, because they get better follow-up service from them?

You may be looking for someone to handle particular accounts so ask some specific questions about their account base.

Q **Who do you sell into currently?**

Q **Who is your main customer?**

⒬ We are looking for someone to handle our . . . account. Have you handled anything similar?

If they are responsible for a sales team you can use the following questions to understand what level of responsibility they have and how they manage targets, under-performers, etc.

⒬ How do you set their targets?

⒬ Is anyone else involved in this?

⒬ Are the team involved?

⒬ How do you keep them motivated?

⒬ How often do you speak to / see their customers?

⒬ How often do you go to customers with them?

⒬ If one of your team is under-performing what do you do?

⒬ Can you give me an example?

⒬ What percentage of your time is spent in the office?

⒬ What do you look for when you are recruiting?

⒬ What mistakes have you made in recruiting? How did you overcome this? How have you changed your recruitment process to ensure this doesn't happen again?

⒬ What successes have you had hiring people?

Questions on technical ability

For junior technical roles you may need to ask straightforward questions about what system they have used and at what level of competence. If you have specified that they must have used a particular system, then your questions will focus specifically around this. In any technical role you do need to be able to appraise exactly what the candidate can do, and therefore a practical task is most appropriate but the following questions will help.

Q What systems do you use / have you used?

Q What training have you had in these?

Q Are you familiar with x that we use here?

Q Can you give me an example where you have used it?

Q Have you developed any systems, and what were they for?

Q Did they work?

Q Have any of them been used elsewhere in the company?

If the candidate has used a system that you are familiar with, you can give them a scenario and ask how they would deal with it.

Questions on their ability to influence others

It is no longer only management jobs where you need to influence people. You may need to be able to influence your team, other departments, other managers, customers, and the list can go on and on. It may even be to persuade the cleaner to empty the rubbish bins even if they have smelly food in them!

it is no longer only management jobs where you need to influence people

Q Who do you have to influence?

This could also apply outside of work.

Q Can you give me an example of how you have influenced a decision within your company?

Q Who did you have to influence in this instance?

Q How did you achieve this?

Q Did it work?

Q Are there any departments / other managers that you have to influence in order to get your job done?

Q How do you deal with this?

Q Can you give me an example to illustrate this?

Questions on leadership skills

Some of the questions looking at leadership are covered under management, but you may be recruiting someone who can lead but who won't be a manager.

Q Are you, or have you ever been, a leader either at work or outside?

Q What kind of leader are you?

Q How would your boss / your team describe your leadership?

Q Is there any way you want to improve your leadership skills?

Q Can you give me an example of where you have had to persuade your team to do something that they didn't agree with? Or that you felt was the wrong way to proceed?

Questions on team work

Working well in a team or successfully managing the team may be an important skill so you need to find out how this candidate copes in that situation. The questions below can be used for team members or team leaders.

Q Do you prefer working on your own or in a team? Why?

If someone doesn't like being in a team this is usually obvious to the other members and can be unproductive.

Q What do you like most about being in this / these teams?

Q What do you like most about leading this / these teams?

Q What do you dislike most?

There may be a particular reason this person does or doesn't like working in a team and it's worth finding out what that is before you discount them as a 'non team player'.

Ⓠ **What other teams are you, or have you been, involved in – for example interdepartmental ones?**

This will show if they work in isolation or are involved in other areas of the business.

Ⓠ **How did you get involved in this?**

If they were nominated by their manager this could indicate that they have some leadership skills, or if they volunteered then they clearly like being in teams and like to be involved in other parts of the business. In the case of a team leader, they may have been promoted into it.

Ⓠ **What have you found most difficult to deal with in the team?**

Use this as a question to lead into the one below. How they dealt with it is more important than what the problem was.

Ⓠ **How did you deal with this?**

Ⓠ **Could it have been dealt with differently? Better?**

These questions will indicate whether or not they are comfortable in a team environment and how they deal with conflict or issues within the team. Did they put forward a reasoned argument and get the team back on track, or go and complain to someone?

Questions on planning skills

There is a certain amount of planning in all jobs. It may be an important factor in your role so you need to establish what the candidate has planned themselves and not as part of a group, or whether they have planned the whole project and not just part of it.

Q Are you responsible for any type of planning within your company? What is this?

Q How have you set about putting a planning schedule together?

Q What factors did you consider?

Q Was anyone else involved?

Q Did the plan work / is the plan working?

Q What difficulties were there getting it operational?

🡕 brilliant summary

- Use the skills identified on the candidate specification to plan your questions.
- Keep delving – make sure you are certain you have the full answer.
- Ask for examples to demonstrate these skills.
- Set scenarios and ask for a reaction.
- Ensure you have enough information to assess the 'essential skills'.

CHAPTER 10

Assessing personality traits

Will they 'fit' into your business?

Once you have planned your strategy for assessing the candidate's skills, move on to plan how you are going to establish if they have the personality traits or qualities that you have identified as necessary to do the job. These are the characteristics you possess inherently and you cannot be trained in. As we considered when putting together the candidate specification, these are more difficult as they can be subjective. You should identify what

> establish if they have the personality traits or qualities that you have identified as necessary

you specifically mean by these qualities and be able to justify why they are important to do the job. Relate them to situations in your company.

Questions to assess whether they are lively, studious, outgoing

You can judge some of these attributes by how the candidate comes across at interview but beware, interviews are very false situations. Candidates react to their interviewer so if you are a relaxed, outgoing person then the candidate is likely to appear like that or behave more like that than perhaps they actually are.

> interviews are very false situations; candidates react to their interviewer

Discuss with them the type of working environment they are in now, and whether they enjoy it.

(Q) Can you tell me about your current / previous working environment, i.e. open-plan office or individual offices?

(Q) How do you find that environment to work in?

(Q) Would you prefer a different one?

It is useful to know if the candidate is used to working in a similar environment to yours, and you can relate other questions specifically to your company.

(Q) We have an open-plan office. Have you worked in that type of office before?

(Q) What do you think are the advantages / disadvantages?

brilliant example

You are recruiting a receptionist for a private hospital. They need to be outgoing as they are dealing with the public, but sensitive and able to deal with patients who are unwell or have just received bad news.

(Q) How would you respond to the above?

(Q) Have you had any similar situations where you have to have a different approach to different people?

If you are still unsure then ask about what they enjoy doing outside of work. Do they go to evening classes or are they out with friends?

Questions to assess their tenacity to get things done

Ask yourself what tasks this candidate may need to perform in your company where they will have to show tenacity. Use these scenarios to ask the candidate what they would do. Are they prepared to keep asking you questions until they can solve the problem, or do they just give up?

 **example**

Staff working in property rental businesses often need to sort out complex queries that may straddle several departments. The sales team have found a new tenant, head office have issued the lease, the reference department have checked references, but the property owner is complaining that they have not received their first rent cheque. How would you sort this out?

The candidate will not know the correct answer because they do not know how your company works, so they will need to ask you questions until they can work it out. You can encourage them further by telling them they can ask as many questions as they like.

Go on to ask them for examples, but make sure you get them to qualify what they are saying.

(Q) What other situations have you had to deal with where you have had to liaise with several other departments?

(Q) Did you solve the query?

(Q) Was anyone else involved?

Questions to establish if they have an eye for detail

Once again, asking the candidate how they would deal with a situation in your own company may work well, and then ask them for further examples.

(Q) Do you spot things that are wrong even if you have not been asked to check them? Such as?

(Q) Can you give me an example of where you have to check things?

Ⓠ What do you have to do?

Ⓠ What sort of mistakes do you find?

This is a good example of where a practical task can work really well.

Questions to assess analytical ability

The best way to appraise this is to set a task. Design a task or several to mirror the kind of analytical duties they would be doing in the job but make sure that it is understandable to someone not working in the company. If speed will be important, put a timeline on the task.

Additionally establish what analysis they do in their current role, and ask for examples.

Ⓠ What are they looking for or producing from the analysis?

Ⓠ How easy is it to find?

Ⓠ What sort of reports (if applicable) do they generate?

Ⓠ Who do these reports go to?

Ⓠ Do they take action on the reports or is this up to someone else?

Questions to assess confidentiality

Confidentiality can play a major part in many different roles. Human Resource positions are perhaps the obvious ones where staff have access to personnel records including salary details. When you hire someone into these roles they will usually have some work experience as it's unlikely that someone straight from education will have the skills needed. Look for candidates who can demonstrate that they can keep confidentiality. Find out first what situations they have been in by asking for general information.

Q Have you ever had to keep confidential information or documents?

Q Was this part of your role when you started with the company?

Very often people are given access to sensitive information once they have been with the company for some time and have 'proven' themselves, so find out if that is the situation with your candidates.

Q Has knowing this information caused you any problems or conflict of interests?

Having this information can sometimes prove to be difficult and it can become a conflict of interest in certain situations.

---

brilliant example

A director is asked by his assistant to sign the order for new office equipment as previously agreed. The director is involved in highly confidential takeover discussions which if they go ahead will result in the office being closed.

The example above can be used as a scenario to ask the candidate how they would react. You are looking for the candidate to come up with a sensitive answer which will stall the order without alerting the assistant to the problem. Set them a situation which could occur in the role you are recruiting, or ask them for an example of where they have had to deal with this and follow with:

Q How would / did you deal with that?

Q Did / would that achieve the outcome you wanted?

Questions to establish honesty

Honesty can be linked with the questions on confidentiality but by honesty we are usually looking for someone involved with something more tangible than for example information. They may be cash handling or have access to goods of some sort. The best solution to this is to take temptation out of people's way and have systems that ensure against dishonesty but this can prove very difficult. Ideally find candidates who can demonstrate that they are honest and trustworthy.

(Q) Have you been in a situation of trust before?

This may not be in a work situation; it could be as treasurer of their local football club for example, but you are looking for someone that other people trust.

(Q) There is a lot of cash in our office so we need people we can trust. Can you give me an example of when you have had to demonstrate your honesty?

(Q) Would your friends describe you as honest? Why?

Questions to establish initiative

If having initiative is one of your criteria, think about the situations in the role you are recruiting where the successful candidate will have to demonstrate they can think on their feet.

Set some real or imaginary situations and ask how they would react.

▶ brilliant example

Your company imports clothing and footwear from around the world, which is mostly transported by sea freight. The products are seasonal and cannot be repeated. You have just had it confirmed that one of the ships from South America, carrying a significant amount of your new season's footwear, ready for launching in two weeks' time, is on fire. What would you do?

There will be different answers to this in different companies, and remember that your interviewee does not know how your systems work. You are looking for someone who can think around the problem and come up with several possible solutions.

Ask them for examples of where they have had to think on their feet and how they made their decision.

Q We are looking for someone who can react quickly in sometimes pressurised situations. Can you give me an example of a situation you have been in where you have had to use your initiative?

The examples they give you may not relate to your company or the way it works, so ask them to detail how they made their decision and quantify their success.

Q How did you make your decision?

Q Can you talk me through your thought process?

Q Did your solution work?

Q Could you have made a better one?

brilliant summary

- Use the personality traits that you identified on the candidate specification to plan your questions.
- Ask for examples from outside of work if necessary.
- Give them a real scenario that you have in your company and ask if they have been in a similar one and what they did.
- Check that you have enough information to assess the 'essential traits'.

CHAPTER 11

Working relationships

Confrontational or compliant

Whatever the job, at whatever level, there will be some working relationships to consider, but how important these are will depend on the role you are recruiting for so decide which of the following are key within your business.

Questions on relationships with managers

The dynamic between direct report and manager will vary enormously. You need to find out how your interviewee responds to their manager and if this approach will work in your company.

> you need to find out how your interviewee responds to their manager

Q How would you describe your working relationship with your boss?

Q How would he / she describe their working relationship with you?

Q Have you ever had a disagreement with a present or previous boss? What was it?

Q How did the two of you overcome it?

Q What is the most frustrating thing about working for your boss?

Q How do you put new ideas forward to your manager?

(Q) How do they react?

(Q) How would you describe your relationship with senior management, i.e. those more senior than your line manager?

Questions on team relationships

Team work is essential in most businesses and therefore so is the relationship within the group and between them and their manager.

(Q) How would you describe your relationship with your peer group / team?

(Q) How would they describe their relationship with you?

(Q) Is there anyone in your team you would like to change?

Relationships with direct reports are also very important so this too needs some investigation.

(Q) How would you describe your relationship with your direct reports?

(Q) What would they say about you?

Most answers to this are 'firm but fair', but ask them to explain and give examples of each.

(Q) How do you motivate your team?

(Q) Give me an example of a problem you have had to deal with within your team.

(Q) How did you deal with it?

(Q) Was that successful?

Questions on external relationships

Working relationships also exist between different departments, other offices and external customers and suppliers.

brilliant example

The facilities manager has hired a very competitively priced cleaning company who started off well but are now slacking. They don't want to lose them because of their price, and they were originally doing a good job.

Ⓠ How do you handle your relationship with customers / suppliers?

Ⓠ What would your customers / suppliers say about you?

Ⓠ Do you have any other external working relationships?

Ⓠ What do you do to develop these relationships?

Ⓠ How successful has this been?

Ⓠ How do you get on with other departments / offices?

Ⓠ What would they say about you?

Ⓠ How do you get them to help you?

Questions on overcoming difficult working relationships

Ⓠ What is the most difficult working relationship you have had to deal with concerning customers / team members / indirect reports / external contacts?

Ⓠ How did you deal with this, and what was the outcome?

Ⓠ Is there anyone in your current or previous roles that you do not get on with?

Ⓠ How did you / how do you deal with this?

Ⓠ Who is the most difficult person you have worked with or for?

Ⓠ How did you overcome this?

If you may have a particularly difficult person in your company you might want to give them as an example and see how the candidate reacts.

There are no right or wrong answers to these questions but you are looking for candidates who are aware of their impact on others and how to deal with people in a variety of situations. You are also looking for positive responses and not just complaints!

brilliant summary

- Concentrate on the most important working relationships for your role.
- Decide if your interviewee handles their relationships appropriately.
- Will their approach work in your company?
- Can they deal with difficult situations and people?

CHAPTER 12

Ambition and motivation

Career progression and reason for application

It's important to establish how ambitious your candidate is and what motivates them so that you can judge if you can match their aspirations. Find out how aggressive their career progression has been and what success they have achieved. What is motivating their application to you, and how keen are they to join your company?

> establish how ambitious your candidate is and what motivates them

Questions on career progression

These questions will not apply to those just leaving education but they will be relevant to everyone else. However, keep in mind that not everyone is career-minded and you may not be looking for someone career-orientated for your vacancy.

(Q) How career-orientated are you, say on a scale of 0–10?

If you are looking for a careerist then establish how career-orientated they think they are and you can then see if they have followed this.

(Q) Highlight where you have moved jobs for career progression.

(Q) Did this pay off?

(Q) I notice the last three jobs that you have had are all the same or similar, so what did you gain from moving companies?

---

brilliant tip

Remember that job titles can be misleading and can mean different things in different companies, so allow your candidate to explain them.

Q What kind of career progression are you looking for here?

If a candidate is exhibiting a high level of ambition you need to ensure you can match that if you hire them.

Q What do you see yourself doing in five years?

Does this fit in with your company's future business plans?

Questions about success

Q How is your success measured?

Success in some roles is easily measured. Salespeople will be deemed a success if they surpass their sales budget, but they may also be evaluated on how many new accounts they have opened, how many additional outlets they are selling into, and so on. By finding out how their success is measured you will learn where the emphasis is in their role, and it will also highlight areas that you may need to probe more. Perhaps opening new accounts is not a key driver for them, but it will be in your company. In some companies they will be measured by key performance indicators (KPIs), as we looked at in Chapter 1.

Q What does success mean to you?

Q Which was your biggest success, and why?

Q What have you gained from your success?

It's useful to know if they are looking for monetary reward or if there is
something else that motivates them.

it's useful to know if they
are looking for monetary
reward or something else

Questions on their reasons for applying for your vacancy

Another interesting point is to ask why the candidate has
applied for your job. You want to know why they are there, and
whether you can meet their expectations.

Q **What made you apply for this particular job?**

Their answer will demonstrate what they know about your
company and whether they have bothered to research it. Junior
candidates may have a more basic approach such as its being
near to their home! At their level that is probably as good a
reason for applying as any.

Keep in mind that if the candidate has been headhunted they
will not consider that they have applied for the job as they have
been directly approached for it, so ask:

Q **What made you decide to come to meet me?**

brilliant tip

With headhunted candidates you will need to 'sell' the job more as
they are not necessarily looking to move.

Q **Are you applying for other jobs? If yes, what? How do they compare
to this one?**

It may be that they have been prompted to apply by your advert
or a headhunt call and you are the only company they are interviewing with. While this is admirable you need to make sure

that they really will leave their current post if you offer them the job so find out what will motivate them to move companies.

(Q) You have been with your present company for six years, so why leave now?

(Q) What will make you decide to move?

(Q) What do you think we can offer you here?

Make sure that their expectations are correct and available.

Questions about their knowledge of your company and market sector

In this day and age of information technology you should expect even the most junior candidate to know something about your company and the more senior ones should be well briefed.

(Q) What do you know about our company? or

(Q) Do you know what our company does?

This may be all you need to ask a junior candidate. It will demonstrate if they have taken the time to prepare for your interview.

Depending on the seniority of the candidate you can use some or all of the following questions to gauge their understanding of your company and its market.

(Q) Our market has shrunk considerably in the last year. Why is that?

(Q) In which other areas do you predict expansion, and why?

(Q) What do you think of our products / services?

(Q) Which do you think is our bestseller?

(Q) Which of our products / services do you think will be our next bestseller?

(Q) Who do you think are our main competitors?

(Q) What do they do better than we do?

(Q) What do we do better than them?

(Q) What markets do we sell in?

(Q) Are you aware how we operate in international markets?

(Q) What are your thoughts on our price structure?

If you are interviewing a candidate from the same sector as your company they should be able to answer these questions through their knowledge of the market. If they are from a different sector they should have done some research, even if they cannot answer in depth.

↗ brilliant summary

- Establish if their ambition matches with what you can offer.
- Discover what motivates them.
- Find out how motivated they are to join you.
- Check if they have researched for their interview.

CHAPTER 13

Senior
candidates

Specialist roles

Most of the questions we have covered will apply to all levels of candidates but the wording may need to be changed depending on the seniority of the candidates. For example in Chapter 6 we looked at finding out about the candidates' duties and asked 'How is your work overseen or checked?' The question is still relevant but for senior candidates you could change it to 'How is success in your role monitored?'

Competence-based questions work well with these candidates but you want more complex and detailed examples than you would expect from less experienced candidates.

> you want more complex and detailed examples than you would expect from less experienced candidates

Questions on specialist roles

For certain specialist roles, especially at more senior levels, you will need to ask specific questions targeted at this experience.

- Firstly find out what they know about this area in your company.
- Question them on their market knowledge and other potential markets.

Q Have they covered this or a similar role in their present or previous jobs?

Q How did they improve what their company was doing? What was the strategy?

Q Who put the strategy together?

Q Were you solely responsible or were others involved?

Q What success did you have?

Q Have you identified any other areas for improvement?

Q What should we do to improve our company?

brilliant example

You are recruiting a new business development manager whose key task will be to develop new markets. Some of the questions below will lead on from general questions about their present and past jobs. They can be used for products or services and for new sectors or international markets.

Q What markets are we in? Are there any other markets you think we should be in?

Q Have you worked in any of these markets?

Q What new markets have you opened?

Q How did you identify the new market?

Q Who else was involved in that process?

Q What strategy did you use?

Q Did you have total responsibility, or were others involved?

Q How successful has this market been?

Ⓠ Is there anything else you could have done to make it more successful?

Ⓠ We are struggling with . . . What would you do to improve that?

These questions will identify if they have ideas on where you can develop and whether they have the experience to do so. They will also help to quantify if their success in new markets is solely down to them or if they are just part of the team involved in it.

Ⓠ Have you identified any gaps in our product range?

Ⓠ Have you launched any new products?

As with looking at new markets, ask them to identify who else was involved, etc., how successful it was and so on, in order to quantify how much of this success was solely down to them.

If you need someone to develop international markets you may need some more specific questions. In some sectors new markets are opened following a chance conversation at a trade show where someone expresses an interest in representing that company. This may be all you are looking for but if you want a more strategic approach use the questions above, and add:

Ⓠ How much research did you do before deciding to launch in a new market?

Ⓠ What research did you look at?

Ⓠ What other factors did you consider?

Ⓠ How much time did you spend in the market prior to launch?

Ⓠ How long do you spend there now?

Ⓠ What is the company structure in that market?

Ⓠ Why have you gone for that option?

Ⓠ What reporting structure is in place?

Q Does that work?

Q What criteria did you use to select your representative there?

Q How do you see that market developing?

you are looking for
good planning strategy,
well thought-out ideas
and success

These questions can apply whether the market is being developed through own company staff, agents, licensees, or distributors. The candidate may not have used the business model that you use or want to use, but you are looking for good planning strategy, well thought-out ideas and success.

Questions on time management

many managers fail
because of their inability to
time-manage multiple
areas of responsibility

Many managers fail because of their inability to time-manage multiple areas of responsibility and cannot delegate efficiently, so you need to understand how this candidate deals with these issues.

Q How do you prioritise your time?

Q What time management techniques work for you?

Q How do you delegate? Talk me through that decision.

Q How do you manage and oversee projects you have delegated?

Q Who takes over while you are away, and how well does that work?

Q What mechanisms do you have in place to deal with the running of the department if you are called away at short notice or off sick?

Questions on influencing and relationships

We have already looked at these areas in earlier chapters but they are even more crucial and far-reaching for senior level employees so you will want to ask more in-depth questions.

Q How do you work with other teams?

Q How do you get other departments to work with you?

Q Who is the most difficult member of your peer group that you have to deal with, and how do you handle that?

There is always a conflict of interest between certain departments such as sales and marketing or buying and merchandising, so get an understanding of how they deal with these. Are they confrontational or quietly influencing?

Q How do you influence the rest of the management team / the board / investors / shareholders?

Q How do you persuade others to support your ideas?

Q How do you motivate your direct reports? Give me an example of where this has / has not worked.

Q What is your relationship with external bodies, e.g. the press?

Q What is the most challenging thing you have had to persuade others to buy into?

Q How did you handle that, and did it work?

Questions on finance

The further up the corporate ladder you climb, the more involved in finance you become. If financial responsibility is part of your job specification then you need to establish how experienced your candidate is in this area and if they are compiling budgets or just working to them.

Q What budgets do you put together? Talk me through the process.

Q How involved is the finance department / company accountant in this? At what stage do they become involved?

Q Can you read a P&L account?

brilliant tip

It's easy to say yes to the above question so check them out with an abridged P&L account.

Q If I show you this one can (P&L account) you tell me what problem areas you can identify?

Q What would you do to rectify these?

Q Are you involved in cash flow projections?

Q How do you forecast these?

Q Are you responsible for setting other budgets? How do you control budgets you have set for others?

Q At what stage do you get involved in negotiations?

Q Who closes the deal?

Q What are the first areas you would look at in a cost cutting exercise?

You need to ensure that their approach will fit in with your company's philosophy.

Questions on strategy planning

At senior levels the role will involve some strategy planning and at more elevated levels this will be a major part of the function.

Q What strategies have you introduced to improve your company's profit in this current climate?

Q Are they working?

Q Were they your ideas or a joint effort?

Q What problems did you inherit when you joined your company, and how did you tackle them?

Q Have you been involved in putting together any emergency strategies?

Q I notice your company has recently made redundancies. Were you involved in that decision? What ramifications did it have on the business?

Q Part of this role is to look at expansion. What ideas do you have?

Q What do you think of our strategy on . . . ?

Q What would you do to enhance that?

Q We are struggling with . . . What strategy would you use to turn that around? Have you been in a similar situation? What did you do?

Q We have recently had bad press over . . . What would you do to overcome that?

Q One of the challenges facing our company is . . . Have you had to deal with that before? What did you do?

Q We are going through a lot of changes including hiring for this new role. Have you had to deal with change management before? How did you deal with that? What were the plus and minus points?

Questions about working across multi functions

You may be looking for a head of department or the equivalent, so although senior in experience they are still specialising in one area but above this level job roles typically become more general and you need to ensure that the candidate can handle this.

Ⓠ Your background is predominantly marketing, but this role will encompass other departments. How will you cope with that?

Ⓠ We are looking for someone to head up sales and marketing. Your background is in sales so how would you handle the marketing team?

Ⓠ Do you think it is right to have one person responsible for these two departments?

Ⓠ What do you see as the advantages / drawbacks?

Ⓠ Heading up several departments can be difficult. Is there an area you would need help in?

Questions on market knowledge

It is these candidates that you will expect to have good market knowledge even if they are in a function that crosses markets, such as finance.

Ⓠ What do you see as the main challenges to our company in this market?

Ⓠ Where do you see our market position?

Ⓠ What is the biggest influence on the market currently?

Ⓠ Who do you consider to be our main competitors?

Ⓠ Which companies do you think compare more favourably than ours? Why? What would you do to change that?

Ⓠ How do you keep abreast of new developments / trends in our market?

Ⓠ What trade events do you go to and what benefit do you gain from these?

Ⓠ What networking groups do you belong to? Have they been advantageous?

You may need to be aware of confidentiality issues at this level, so make sure the scenarios you are giving are in the public domain and that the questions you are asking are not going to be off limits for discussion. Equally be very wary of the candidate who is prepared to give away what amounts to trade secrets or to break confidences!

brilliant summary

- Concentrate on competence-based questions with detailed examples.
- Check that their organisation and time management skills will allow them to cope with your job.
- Ensure that they are able to work across multi functions.
- Make sure they have the strategy planning skills and experience that you need.
- Establish their market knowledge.

CHAPTER 14

Closing the interview

Final questions and assessing the candidate

Questions on salary and travelling may have been covered earlier, but if not, ensure you ask for this information now. You will then need some time to give the candidate more information on the role and answer their questions before finally assessing them.

Questions about travelling and re-location

It is worth covering any travel or location issues before deciding on which candidates to take to the next stage, as these can often be the reasons for offers being turned down.

If your interviewee is living some distance away then find out how carefully they have thought about their travel arrangements. Junior-level candidates can sometimes make some very optimistic assumptions about travel times.

travel or location issues can often be the reasons for offers being turned down

brilliant tip

Be wary of candidates who currently drive ten minutes to work but now think they can commute for one and a half hours on public transport. In many cases they will find this is exhausting and often decide to leave.

Q I notice that your last job was very local to you, but this company is the other side of town. How are you going to get here?

Q We do not have parking facilities, so have you checked how you will get here?

At senior levels you may be seeing candidates who will have to re-locate if you offer them a job. If you were aware that your applicants would be applying from across the country or even internationally then you should have included the cost of a re-location package in your recruitment budget.

Re-locating staff can become very complicated, especially if they need to sell their current home and buy another property. They may well have children in school in a crucial year who cannot be moved immediately or a partner who cannot re-locate because of their job.

brilliant tip

Offers that include re-locating are often declined because the candidate's partner is not totally in favour of the move. Try finding a way of having a conversation with the partner to assess their thoughts on re-locating.

Keep to open questions and avoid making assumptions.

Q What would you do about re-locating if we offered you the job?

Q Have you looked at the price of property / rents near here?

Q You mentioned your partner; will they re-locate with you?

Q Are there any other factors affecting your re-location?

You want to make sure that they have thought this through at this stage, not later.

Travelling may be part of the job that you are recruiting for and you need to make candidates aware of this and to ensure they can meet this requirement. State what they will need to do and why, so it is clear that this is a necessity of the job.

brilliant example

'You have a lot of liaison with our London office and you will need to attend the regular monthly meeting which will involve staying overnight.'

Or:

'We source most of our product from China and you will need to spend ten days there every three months.'

Q Do you have any problems meeting this requirement?

Q Do you have a similar situation currently?

brilliant tip

Make sure you ask ALL candidates the same questions in the same way. Do not confine these questions to women whom you assume have child care issues. This will be discriminatory.

Questions about salary and notice period

It is vital to make sure you have a good understanding of what the candidate is currently earning but at this point salary packages can become 'enhanced' perhaps with bonuses added in and so on, so you need to ensure you receive a complete breakdown.

make sure you have a good understanding of what the candidate is currently earning

(Q) What is your current (or 'your last', if they are not working) basic salary?

(Q) Do you get a bonus and / or commission?

(Q) How much did you earn in total last year?

Always ask them to quantify bonuses or commissions. Just having a bonus potential does not mean you earn it. Find out if they are due to be paid any bonuses and whether handing in their notice would affect this. (This may result in their wanting to defer their resignation, or you may have to buy them out of their bonus – see Chapter 15, The Offer). If you are still not sure that you are getting the true picture, ask:

(Q) What does your last P60 state that you earned? / Is that what it states on your P60?

(Q) Do you have a company pension, and what are the company's contributions? Is it a final salary scheme?

do not forget to ask for their notice period; it can be several months

If they have a final salary pension you may not be able to match it, so you will have to build something else into any offer.

Finally do not forget to ask for their notice period; do not assume that it will be a month, as it can be several months and more for high-level candidates.

(Q) What is your notice period?

(Q) Is that negotiable, as we really want someone sooner?

(Q) We have an important meeting next month. If you were offered the job, could you attend?

These two questions help you to plan accordingly but they also demonstrate the candidate's level of interest in the job.

Giving the candidate information

Many candidates come out of an interview without knowing anything more about the job or the company because the interviewer has forgotten to include this or they have simply run out of time.

An interview is a two-way process – you are making a decision but so is the candidate. Many interviewers assume that the candidates are desperate to accept the job and forget they have a choice and are likely to be applying for other jobs too. If you want them to join your company, you need to make them really interested and 'sell' it to them.

You can let them know of any future company plans, how the company has grown or how the role they are applying for could develop. If the person you are replacing has been promoted, tell the applicants – it's good news!

> if you want them to join your company 'sell' it to them

If there are any negatives you should also disclose them. Most candidates will respond to this honesty and if they are currently working in your market sector they are likely to be aware of any problems you are having. Explain what the problems are and most importantly what you are doing to counteract them.

Final questions – yours and theirs

At the end of any interview always inform the candidate what will happen next and in what timescale. Make sure you have discussed your company and the job fully, including salary package.

If this is a candidate you think you are interested in, then ask them what their thoughts are.

Ⓠ Are you interested in going to the next stage?

Ⓠ If we offered you the job, would you take it?

> ## ☀ **brilliant** tip
>
> Unless you are absolutely sure about your decision, be careful not to
> make this sound like an offer. People often hear what they want to
> hear and this can lead to disappointment. Tell them if you have
> other candidates to see or if you need to discuss the ones you have
> seen with other people.

It is worth knowing how they will respond and it gives you the
chance to answer any of their questions or doubts, or you can ask:

Ⓠ Do you have any other questions?

Ⓠ Do you have any reservations about our company or the job?

This can throw up some difficult questions for you to respond
to such as:

Ⓠ Why is this job vacant?

Ⓠ Why is the person in this role leaving?

These are the most common end-of-interview questions and
you need to give an honest, but whenever you can positive,
answer. Explain why the person is leaving – they have been here
three years but now wanted to train to be a teacher. The fact
they have been there three years is a positive point.

Ⓠ Why are you recruiting externally – don't you promote from within?

Ⓠ There are rumours that you are making people redundant. Are they
true, and how will this affect this role?

Ⓠ You have re-structured several times recently. Why is this?

Ⓠ Your company has been getting very bad press because . . . Why is this and what are you doing about it?

Remember that despite these issues this candidate has attended the interview so they are still interested in your company. Again give them an honest answer. All companies have problems but the candidate needs to understand the reasons for them and what has been done to resolve the issues.

Ⓠ What are my chances of being offered this job?

Ⓠ How do I compare with other candidates?

Unless you are very sure about this candidate, keep your answer neutral by saying:

'It is difficult to say, as I still have other people to see', or 'It's difficult to say because we have had such good applicants and we are still interviewing.'

You may have a clear 'favourite' amongst your candidates but it is worth reviewing and marking each one to ensure that you select the one most suited to your role.

You may also have included psychometric or other types of testing or a practical task, so make sure that these are evaluated alongside your interview assessment before making your final decision.

Assess the candidates

At the end of your interviews you must assess the candidates and decide which to take to the next stage or to make an offer to.

Using the points system, as discussed earlier, is a useful tool at all stages and will ensure you have a uniform and fair system for evaluating applicants. We looked at awarding five points for each 'essential' skill, two for 'desirable' and one for 'useful'. You can adjust this in any way you want, but ensure the points are heavily weighted for the essential skills.

Write up your interview notes. If you are new to interviewing or do not do it very often, it is very easy to confuse candidates and forget the details. Include any areas you want to investigate at the next interview.

If more than one person has been involved the ideal situation is to assess the candidates individually and then compare notes.

Decide on which candidates to take to the next stage, remembering to highlight any areas that need probing further or points that you have not yet covered.

Split decisions

If you are in the lucky position of coming to the end of your selection process but have two or more candidates that you can't decide between, then what do you do?

This situation is unlikely and usually means that the candidates have simply not been assessed in enough detail, so ask yourself the following:

Q Have they met ALL the 'essential' criteria?

Q Which 'desirable' criteria does each one have?

Q Finally, which 'useful' criteria do they have?

You may now have identified a point of difference between the candidates or you may have found that you had not investigated all of these areas.

Go back to the candidates and ask them about the areas you missed. This could be done by telephone or through your recruitment consultant, or you may decide to ask them back for another interview.

 **tip**

Be cautious about calling candidates back for unscheduled interviews. This can make them 'cool off' as you or your company can be seen as indecisive.

If you do opt for another meeting, then explain why.

Plan the meeting so that you ensure that you will get the information you need.

Q What will you ask?

Q Is there anyone else they should meet? Maybe someone was away from the business when the interviews were being conducted or there is another member of the team that they will interface with. This will also be another view on deciding between the two.

Q Can you think of some more situations that you want them to discuss?

Alternatively could you introduce another element in the decision making such as psychometric testing, a task or a trial afternoon if they have not already been carried out?

What about the obvious? Is one looking for a more realistic salary than the other, or does one have a more workable notice period than the other? These are not in themselves reasons to hire or not to hire someone, but if it's still a split decision then factor this in.

Finally, if you still have two identically matched individuals then in these circumstances you *can* hire the one you like best!

brilliant summary

- Make sure you have salary and notice period information.

- Make sure they have enough information to decide if they want to take their application further.

- Establish if they are going on to other interviews and where they are in this process. Don't lose them.

- Explain to them what will happen next and give a timeline.

- Assess the candidate – are you taking them to the next stage?

- Highlight any areas to be covered at the next meeting.

PART 3

After the interviews

CHAPTER 15

The offer

How to make sure the candidate takes the job

Now that you have decided which candidate is the most suitable for your role you will want to make them an offer. It is important to get this right. If the selected candidate turns you down you may need to start the whole process again, which will be time-consuming and costly.

If you have a second candidate who is a close contender, consider if you will offer them the job if your first choice declines. Explain to them that there will be a delay in making a decision. Perhaps a key decision maker is away, for example. Do not tell them they are second choice as psychologically you want them to think they are exactly what you are looking for, should you decide to offer them the job.

> if the selected candidate turns you down you may need to start the whole process again

By this stage you should be aware of what is motivating the candidate to seek new employment and join your company. This motivation is usually complex and is unlikely to be purely based on money, but this will play a big part and you need to make the offer as appealing as possible.

 **tip**

Beware of candidates claiming they are not looking for an increase in salary because they want to join your company for other reasons. Very few people will change jobs without an increase.

How to structure the offer

In larger organisations salary and benefits will be pre-set and the candidates will already have been told what the package is, but in many companies there is some flexibility.

Before you can put together your offer you need to make sure you have the candidate's full present salary and benefits, which will include some or all of the following:

- Basic salary.
- Personal bonuses (those based on individual performance) – how they are calculated and how much they have earned.
- Group bonuses (based on team effort).
- Company bonuses (based on company performance).
- Commission – how it is calculated and how much they earn from it.
- Pension plan – does it include employer contribution? Is it a final salary pension?
- Other benefits such as private health care for self or self and dependants, or discounts on products – how much, what on, and how much does this save the candidate?
- Car – what type.
- Car allowance – how much.
- Private mileage.
- Any benefits to spouse/partner.

- Holidays.
- Sick pay.
- Shares / share options – what do they have currently and what will happen to the shares when they leave?

There will be other considerations for those working offshore but these will not be comparable to locally-based jobs. They will only be relevant if your role is also offshore. These packages vary so you will need to know if theirs covers housing, car with driver, schooling for children, flights home, etc.

brilliant tip

If you are using a recruitment consultant they should be able to provide you with the details of the candidate's package and give you some indication of what they are looking for in terms of salary, bonuses, etc.

Basic salary

Basic salary is usually the most important component as you can't pay your mortgage with pension contributions or other benefits, so most candidates will be looking for an increase in this.

brilliant tip

The majority of people leave for an overall increase of around 20%, so try and structure your offer to cover this.

Bonuses and commissions

Bonuses and commissions are only worth what they pay out, so make sure you know how much the candidate has actually earned and not what they could have done if they had reached full bonus.

 **example**

A candidate tells you that they can earn up to 30% of their salary in a company bonus scheme. However, this is based on company profitability and in the last two years the company has not been in profit and the bonus has not been paid at all.

Equally, make sure you can quantify your own bonus schemes. Have some examples of what individuals have earned, levels of company bonus, when they are paid and any qualifying periods,

make sure you can quantify your own bonus schemes

for example in some cases you may have to work a full year before you qualify for the company annual bonus whereas in others it will be paid pro rata.

Find out when the candidate's bonuses and commissions are due. It can be a stumbling block if a candidate realises that they will not be paid a bonus if they leave before a certain date. This may mean that they will want to start later than anticipated. In the case of a more senior employee you may want to offer a 'signing-on bonus' if the candidate agrees to start when you need them to and to forego their bonus or commission.

If the candidate has been earning commission or bonuses which are not replicated in your offer, make sure you include something else to compensate.

Pension benefits

Candidates at all levels have become much more aware of the benefits of company pensions. If you are hiring someone with a company pension, especially if it is a final salary scheme, but your business does not have one or yours is not comparable, you may need to increase your offer on basic to cover this shortfall.

If you are offering a pension plan with employer contributions, make sure you have all the details.

Other benefits

You do not have to match the exact benefits the candidate has but you will need to equal them or surpass them in value in some way. Whatever your company benefits are, make sure you can explain and quantify them.

Medical insurance is one benefit that many candidates do not want to have to give up if they change jobs despite the fact that the monetary advantage to them after tax is quite small. For the same reason it is also a useful tool to add into your offer as the perceived value is high.

Do not forget to include company facilities such as a heavily subsidised canteen or a free in-house gym. Although these are not financial payments they will represent substantial savings if they are not available in the candidate's current workplace.

Car or car allowance

Because of the tax implications company cars are no longer the benefit they used to be and many companies now opt for car allowances as they are easier to administer.

If you are recruiting a candidate who currently has a company car or allowance but you do not offer one, you will need to compensate in some other way and ideally on the basic.

be aware that in some sectors company cars are still seen as status symbols

Be aware that in some sectors company cars are still seen as status symbols and candidates may be disinclined to downgrade.

If you are offering a car allowance, especially to a candidate who has never had one, make sure they understand that this is taxed as part of their salary.

Benefits to spouse or partner

Some benefits will cover the spouse or partner of your new employee. Medical insurance may be for the employee only or may include dependants.

If you offer any benefits here make sure they are offered to all the relevant people and that you are not discriminating against single-sex couples, for example.

Holidays

The legal minimum holiday entitlement is now 5.6 times the usual working week so for a five-day week this works out to 28 days. This is including the eight statutory bank holidays.

In some sectors or for senior level roles it is more likely that the norm will be five weeks. If this is the case in your sector, then you should consider increasing your holiday entitlement as you will find that candidates are very loath to give up any holiday allowance and drop from five to four weeks' holiday per annum.

Sick pay

The offer of sick pay schemes and the level of entitlements are rarely deal-breakers at the offer stage. It may be that there is a reticence among applicants to ask for too many details in case they sound as if they will be taking time off work.

You do not have to offer a company sick pay scheme but if you do, explain how this operates as it can be a significant benefit especially if the candidate is not in a scheme at present.

Share / share options

At senior levels shares or options to buy shares at a preferential rate can be a very attractive feature.

Once again make sure you have the details of your plan to hand, especially for more junior candidates who may not have had this option before.

If you are offering a job to someone who currently has shares in their present company, you need to ensure that they know the implications of leaving that business. In some cases they may lose their shares or at least not be able to cash them in, and this may need to be factored into your offer.

Re-location costs

If you are expecting a candidate to re-locate in order to take up your offer of employment you will need to offer some kind of re-location package. In larger companies this will be calculated by a set formula but if you are a smaller company or this is the first time you have had to re-locate someone then you will need to put one together.

Unless you are planning or see a need to re-locate on a regular basis then the easiest option is to deal with it on an individual basis. Find out what the individual plans to do. Will they keep their main home but rent locally, or will they want to sell up and buy again?

Re-locating is fraught with problems. There is a huge variance in the price of homes in different parts of the country, which may mean that for the price of a large four-bedroom family home in Yorkshire for example they will have to consider a much smaller apartment in central London. Also it is not always easy to sell a property and they may have to rent for some time.

The candidate should not be out of pocket by re-locating to join your company, so you could consider including the following in your re-location package:

- Removal costs.
- Legal fees for buying and / or selling their main property.
- Rental allowance for a set interim period between buying and selling their home.
- Interest payments on a bridging loan to facilitate the purchase of a property while trying to sell theirs.
- Stamp duty.
- An allowance for carpets and curtains.

Most companies offer a one-off payment, which is tax free up to a current limit of £8,000 and can only be used to cover these costs on production of relevant receipts or invoices. Any amounts over this limit will be classed as income and liable to tax and National Insurance contributions.

Many candidates will not want to re-locate completely, especially if they have children at school or their spouse or partner has a job they do not want to leave. You need to consider if this will work for your business and what, if any, re-location package you want to offer in these circumstances.

Review your offer

Finally, review your offer and make sure it is going to be tempting. It has got to be worth the candidate's moving companies for.

 **brilliant** tip

When offering a different type of role, money may be less important, but few will accept without an increase in salary.

If you have a flexibility, consider if there is another way you could structure the offer to make it more interesting for this particular candidate. Could you include an additional benefit that they do not have currently?

 **brilliant** example

Private health care is a relatively inexpensive perk but is considered highly attractive, as is an extra week's holiday.

If you are putting these into an offer but they are not your company norm, be aware of how this could impact on other staff. If this is a new role or this is the only person at a certain level then this will not be a problem, but if they are part of a team you will have to offer these benefits to the others. People do talk about their salary packages.

How to make the offer

Verbal offer

In the first instance, make the offer verbally. Make sure you have all of the terms to hand so you can discuss them with the candidate. This will help you get immediate feedback and will alert you to any potential problems.

Candidates are likely to be at work, so ideally make the call out of hours or call and ask the candidate when it will be a good time to talk to them in detail. Ask for their immediate thoughts but allow them time to think the offer over. Agree a time by which they will get back to you with an answer.

If you are working with a recruitment consultant they will make the offer for you. It is often easier to make the offer through a third party, especially if there is likely to be some negotiation. However, if this becomes prolonged or complicated it might be preferable to cut out the middleman and speak directly to the candidate yourself. You can then gauge their feedback and it may enable you to structure the offer differently.

Once you have made the offer, make sure the offer letter is sent out immediately even if the candidate has not yet accepted. There is nothing more frustrating than being offered a job and then waiting days for the written confirmation.

If the candidate turns down your offer, make sure you find out why. There may be something in the offer that you can change to make it more interesting, or there may be something they have doubts over and you can put their mind at rest.

The offer letter

Candidates will expect to see your offer in writing, and if they are in employment they will want to agree the terms of the offer before they resign. You cannot expect anyone to resign with just a verbal offer. Also, it is a legal requirement to issue a written statement of employment within the first two months of the new employee starting work so it will be easier to do it at this stage.

The offer letter should include the following:

- the job title and the fact that you are offering them that job
- any pre-conditions which the offer is subject to, such as exam results
- any post conditions such as being subject to a satisfactory probation period
- salary and how it is paid, e.g. last working day of the month into a bank account

- bonuses and commission
- hours of work
- any other benefits
- pension arrangements
- holiday entitlement
- place of employment
- the starting date
- what action the candidate needs to take, e.g. returning a signed acceptance of the offer, agreement to references being taken up, any date constraints on acceptance
- request for bank details and national insurance number (you may want these sent to you or you may ask for them on the first day)
- instruction to bring their P45 if they have one on the first day.

The offer letter can form the main terms and conditions of employment but some companies will have detailed contracts of employment and it is good practice to send these out with the offer letter if possible.

If the contract is going to be issued later, then you should state that in your offer letter. You should also make it clear if the offer letter is going to form part of that contract as there are points in it that are not specifically covered in the main contract.

If you do not have contracts of employment it is worth taking legal advice and considering having one put together. In most cases one contract can cover all types and levels of job up to senior management, where there may be significant differences in the terms and conditions.

Remember that the employment contract is a legal one, and exists even before the candidate has commenced employment.

Start date

Once they have accepted, you need to agree a start date. This should fit in with their resignation period but it also needs to fit in with your plans. There may be a particular meeting you need them to attend or they may need to start when you are available or other key people are in the business. If they have a long notice period you can always ask if they can attend an important event before they start.

brilliant tip

Most employers think immediately about having a new recruit start on a Monday. Sometimes a Wednesday or Thursday start may be more beneficial. It gives the new member of staff two or three days to settle in, then a weekend break ready to start fresh the following week.

Ask them to start a little later on their first morning. This allows whoever is doing the induction to get the rest of their day sorted out. This will be especially important if this is a line manager who needs to fit the induction around their normal working week and regular commitments.

Induction programme

Starting a new job is daunting for everyone, no matter how senior, and it can be especially nerve-racking for junior employees.

The aim of the induction programme is:

- to help new employees settle in as rapidly as possible
- to give a good impression of your company
- to make them feel welcome.

 **tip**

The quicker they settle in, the quicker they will be working at full capacity. Therefore consider it time well spent.

In larger companies the induction programmes will be devised and organised by the human resource team but they are equally important in smaller businesses.

If you are putting together an induction for the first time, remember you will be able to use it for other new starters but make sure you review it each time to ensure that the details have not changed. It can be conducted by the line manager or you could allocate this responsibility to another member of staff.

Give the new employee a copy of the induction programme, especially if it is over several days or involves training sessions.

brilliant tip

Start by asking yourself what you would need to know if you were starting in your company for the first time.

General inductions for all staff should include some or all of the following:

- Paperwork / identity card. There are usually some formalities to complete on the first day. You will need bank details and national insurance numbers if you do not already have them, and P45 if available.
- Site orientation – in smaller companies show new employees around the whole site, or in larger companies familiarise them with the area they will be working in and around.

- Include where to leave their belongings and where the toilets are.

- Health and safety. If you are in an area where there are hazards such as chemicals, or on a building site, you should ask the new recruit to sign to say that you have given them health and safety training.

- Other people – introduce them to the other key people that they will be working with or need to interact with.

- Canteen or lunch arrangements. If you do not have a company canteen, explain what most people do for lunch and where it can be eaten.

- Telephone training. One of the most frustrating things about being in a new environment is not knowing how to answer the phone. Include training on how to answer a call, how to transfer, put on hold and if the calls are external what wording the company prefers staff to answer with.

- Emergency procedures. In all organisations this should include evacuation procedures, location of alarms, fire extinguishers and fire exits. In others this may be more extensive, such as in a hospital or other areas with responsibility for members of the public.

- There is also likely to be other training specific to their job which will need to take place over a period of days, including computer system, procedures and so on. Do not try to fit everything in a short period of time; people can only take in so much and you will end up spending time repeating things. Training can take place over the first week or even longer if necessary.

- The induction for more senior employees should include the above but they will need to spend more time meeting other people and understanding how their role relates, what their departments do, and this can also be covered over a few days.

brilliant tip

Include a review at the end of the first day, the first week, and the first month in your induction programme. Do not assume everything is going well – make sure it is.

Another useful way of helping employees fit in is to have a 'buddying' system. This is where one person, usually from the new employee's peer group, becomes a buddy to them to help them settle in and answer their questions for them. This can take the pressure off the line manager and the new person will feel comfortable asking their buddy more basic questions like where to get stationery from, rather than bothering their manager.

brilliant summary

- Make sure you know exactly what their current or last salary package is.
- Structure your offer to make it tempting.
- Take their benefits package into account.
- Make the offer verbally but put it in writing immediately.
- Arrange a mutually convenient start date and make sure the relevant people will be on your premises.
- Devise an induction programme to help the new employee settle in as quickly as possible to enable them to start working to full capacity.

CHAPTER 16

Discrimination

What is discrimination?

The majority of interviewers are fair-minded people who simply want to find the right person for the job, and most applicants just want to do their best in the selection process. As you are not a person that discriminates you may feel you don't need to read on, but are you sure that you are aware of the following:

Q You are such a competent interviewer that you are positive that you never ask discriminatory questions or make such comments?

Q All of your recruitment processes are fair and do not include any wording or criterion that could discriminate?

Q Others involved in the process are also fair-minded and aware of your company equal opportunities policy if you have one?

Q You are aware of both direct discrimination, which is often obvious and more easily identified, and the more difficult to identify indirect discrimination?

Q Discrimination can be against an individual because of whom they associate with, including friends and family?

Q It is unlawful to instruct or put pressure on others to discriminate?

Ⓠ Exactly what discrimination covers, which now includes:

- Sex, including marital status
- Race
- Disability
- Age
- Sexual orientation
- Religion or belief.

The Acts, Rules and Codes of Practice that govern discrimination are detailed and complex and cover people from the application stages through to and during employment and affect decisions on promotion, training, redundancies, in fact every aspect of employment. Human Resource practitioners in your company will be able to advise you on these and it is their responsibility to ensure that good practice is adhered to. If you are in a small business without the benefit of in-house experts, it is worth familiarising yourself with the legislation via the various government websites, and if there are areas that you are still unsure of then take professional advice.

Remember, the primary responsibility legally rests with each employer to ensure that there is no unlawful discrimination.

One of the points that the various codes of practice and guidelines relating to the above all state is that it is good practice for companies to have an Equal Opportunities Policy. This sets out the company's approach to each of these and the methods they have in place to ensure that discrimination does not take place during the recruitment process and in the workplace. It is also recommended that applicants are monitored to ensure that your methods of sourcing candidates are producing applications from all backgrounds, ages, races and so on, and if this is not the case then you adapt your methods to encourage this.

Equal Opportunity Policies are usually set out by expert human resource practitioners and often there is not the expertise to devise these in-house, especially in smaller companies.

If you do not have such a policy, then work to the guidelines that opportunities for employment should be equally open to all eligible candidates, and selection should be based solely on merit. No applicant should be placed at a disadvantage by rules, requirements, conditions or practices that have a disproportionately adverse effect on his or her group.

Below is a guide on the types of discrimination there are, what you should be aware of in the recruitment process, some of the pitfalls and how to avoid them.

Discrimination legislation

In brief, there is legislation on each of the following:

Sex discrimination

The Sex Discrimination Act prohibits discrimination against men, as well as against women, and also requires that married people should not be treated less favourably than single people of the same sex.

It is unlawful to select candidates on the ground of sex except for certain jobs when a person's sex is a genuine occupational qualification (known as GOQ) for that job. There are very few instances in which a job will qualify for a GOQ on the grounds of sex but these may arise, for example, where considerations of privacy and decency or authenticity are involved.

But beware, a GOQ will not be valid where members of the appropriate sex are already employed in sufficient numbers to meet the employer's likely requirements without undue inconvenience.

 **example**

In a job where sales assistants may be required to undertake changing room duties, it might not be lawful to claim a GOQ in respect of all the assistants on the grounds that any of them might be required to undertake changing room duties from time to time. The argument would be that at any one time there would be staff of the right sex to wait on customers in the changing room.

The Sex Discrimination Act also expressly states that the need of the job for strength and stamina does not justify restricting it to men.

A job for which a GOQ was used in the past should be re-examined if the post falls vacant again, to see whether the GOQ still applies. Circumstances may well have changed, rendering the GOQ inapplicable.

Race discrimination

The Race Relations Act makes it illegal to discriminate against, or harass, applicants for employment on the grounds of colour or nationality or ethnic, racial, or national group.

This discrimination could occur when an applicant is treated less favourably than another in similar relevant circumstances on the grounds of his or her colour, race, nationality, ethnic or national origins.

Indirect, but still illegal, discrimination can also occur because of these attributes in someone related to the candidate or associated with him or her.

take legal advice on whether you can use positive discrimination and how to do so

In certain circumstances you can take positive action to attract applicants from groups that are under-represented in your work-force. If you think this is the case in your company, then take legal advice on whether you can use positive discrimination and how to do so in order to attract candidates from these groups.

Disability discrimination

The Disability Discrimination Act protects disabled people from discrimination in the workplace. The Act's definition of a disabled person is one who 'has a physical or mental impairment which has a substantial and long-term adverse effect on his ability to carry out normal day-to-day activities'.

Smaller companies used to be exempt from this Act but this is no longer the case and the Act now applies to companies regardless of how many employees they have.

Employers are also obliged to make 'reasonable adjustments' in order to allow disabled people to work. These include measures to ensure that a disabled job applicant is not at a disadvantage compared with an able-bodied person, and include adjustments to the workplace to accommodate a disabled person. The employer's size and resources will be taken into account when judging whether adjustments are, or would be, 'reasonable'.

There are a lot of assumptions and stereotypical ideas about disabled people, so do not assume that:

- Because a person does not look disabled, he / she is not disabled.
- Most disabled people use wheelchairs.
- People with learning disabilities cannot be valuable employees, or that they can only do low-status jobs.
- A person with a mental health problem cannot do a demanding job.
- All blind people read Braille or have guide dogs.

- All deaf people use sign language.
- Because a disabled person may have less employment experience (in paid employment) than a non-disabled person, they have less to offer.

The Disability Discrimination Act requires employers to think about ways of complying with their legal duties. Listening carefully to disabled people and finding out what they want will help employers to meet their obligations by identifying the best way of meeting disabled people's needs.

These discussions should take place early on in the recruitment process. Discussing with disabled people what is required to meet their needs will reassure an employer that suitable adjustments can be carried out cheaply and with very little inconvenience.

Age discrimination

The Employment Equality (Age) Regulations make it unlawful to discriminate against job applicants because of their age. Even if you do not know the applicant's actual age, discrimination can be claimed to have taken place if your decision is based on your perceived age of the applicant.

Ensure that you take off any age-related questions on application forms or other literature and avoid age-related questions or comments during the interview.

Sexual orientation

The Employment Equality (Sexual Orientation) Regulations make it illegal to discriminate on grounds of orientation towards persons of the same sex (lesbians and gays), the opposite sex (heterosexuals) and the same and opposite sex (bisexuals).

These regulations also cover discrimination on the grounds of perceived as well as actual sexual orientation, and being discriminated against on grounds of the sexual orientation of those you associate with, such as friends and family.

Religion or belief

The Employment Equality (Religion or Belief) Regulations relate to discrimination on the grounds of religion, religious belief or similar philosophical belief, and the definition of 'religion or belief' is defined as *any* religion, religious belief or similar philosophical belief.

You are not allowed to treat someone less favourably because of your own religion or belief.

This also covers discrimination in relation to perceived religion, assuming correctly or incorrectly that someone has a particular religion or belief, as well as actual religion or belief. These Regulations, like those covering sexual orientation and race, also cover being discriminated against on grounds of the religion or belief of those with whom you associate.

Direct and indirect discrimination

All of the Acts and Regulations covering discrimination include provisions for direct and indirect discrimination.

Direct discrimination is more obvious and more easily avoided. It can occur when an applicant is treated less favourably than another in a similar situation on the grounds of one of the above forms of discrimination. This can include actual or assumed facts.

Assumed facts for example can include treating someone unfairly because of their age even though you do not actually know their age, or assuming someone is not British because they do not comply with your idea of a stereotypical British person. You cannot claim you were not discriminating because you didn't know, because it may be proven that you were discriminating because you had assumed.

 **examples**

- Treating an applicant less favourably because they are, or appear to be, over fifty and you want to hire someone in their mid twenties because you have a young team.

- You have a shortlist of two candidates, one male and one female, and you hire the man for no other reason than you think he will have less time off because he is not responsible for children.

- You decide not to hire a disabled person because you do not want to get involved in having to adapt the equipment they need to use.

Indirect discrimination is more subtle but still illegal. It can occur if you put a criterion into your selection process that on the face of it may not appear discriminatory but that will put certain people at a disadvantage to others and you cannot justify the reason for it. It may apply equally to every applicant but it can only be met by a smaller proportion of people from a particular group.

brilliant **example**

This could be asking for fluent written English when there is no requirement or need for writing English in the job. This will prejudice non-native speakers and you cannot justify why you have asked for it.

How to avoid discrimination

All of the legislation has recommendations for how to avoid discrimination during the selection process, most of which is common sense and by being aware of it you will be able to plan your recruitment fairly and in a non-discriminatory way.

brilliant tips

- Plan your recruitment process so that it is fair to everyone.
- Use the same recruitment process for everyone.
- Give all applicants the same information.
- Do not make assumptions or stereotypes (for example that only men can do certain manual jobs, or people of a certain age may not be capable of learning new computer systems).
- Treat all applicants in the same way.
- Ensure that all applications are processed in the same way whether they are from men or women, age groups, etc.
- Ensure the duties and tasks that are in the job specification are necessary to complete the job satisfactorily.
- Ensure any selection criteria are fair and not prejudiced against any particular group of applicants.
- Make sure others involved in the recruitment process understand the company policies on discrimination, and provide training if needed to ensure their judgements are objective.
- Plan your interview.
- Do not ask questions that you would not expect to be asked or want to answer yourself.
- Avoid discriminatory comments even if they are meant harmlessly.
- Base your decisions about recruitment on the skills required to do the job.
- Keep records of interviews, where practicable, showing why applicants were or were not appointed.

Identifying the needs of the business – job specifications

The various regulations and codes of practice recommend that employers prepare a job specification for any vacant post.

As we discussed in Chapter 1, the job specification is a useful tool in the recruitment process and by ensuring that it is written in a non-discriminatory way it will help ensure that you do not discriminate when you are selecting and hiring new employees.

Once you have compiled your job specification, re-read it to make sure it is not discriminatory and ask yourself the following:

Ⓠ Is it written plainly in English (or Welsh in Wales)?

Ⓠ Is it jargon-free?

Ⓠ Is each duty or task on the specification necessary to complete the job satisfactorily?

Ⓠ Are you able to justify each one as being necessary and that it does not overstate a duty, or the responsibilities attached to it? (If you include a task or duty that is not necessary or its relevance is overstated you could be discriminating against certain groups that cannot match that requirement and therefore it could be seen as discrimination.)

Ⓠ Have you made it as clear as possible what the job entails? To help with clarity it may be useful to describe the duties and the tasks a person would be expected to carry out over a certain period of time, for example an average working day / week / month.

Identifying the candidate – the candidate specification

In Chapter 2 we looked at drawing up a candidate or person specification describing the skills, knowledge, abilities, qualifications, and experience and qualities that are considered necessary or desirable in a candidate, in order to perform all the duties in the job specification satisfactorily. This is recommended to ensure candidates and those involved in the recruitment process are aware of what is needed to do the job.

To avoid claims that a candidate specification includes potentially discriminatory requirements, criteria or conditions, once you have written it ask yourself the following questions:

(Q) Have you included only the criteria needed to perform the duties in the job description satisfactorily?

(Q) Are the requirements at the right level? For example, by calling for 'excellent knowledge of English' when 'good understanding' is more appropriate.

(Q) Are the qualifications you have asked for necessary, appropriate and still current? Do not ask for higher qualifications than are actually needed to do the job satisfactorily.

(Q) Educational and vocational qualifications have changed and developed over the years, so is it clear that you will accept relevant alternatives? For example the recognised personnel qualification used to be the IPM (Institute of Personnel Management) but is now the CIPD (Chartered Institute of Personnel Diploma).

(Q) Have you made sure that the qualifications you specify are not disadvantaging people at different ages? Candidates over 50 are less likely to have a degree than younger candidates, because fewer people went to university at that time. Therefore by asking for a degree when it is not strictly necessary you may be prejudicing more mature candidates.

(Q) Are there other ways of specifying the skill level you require rather than through qualifications?

(Q) If you are going to be specific about qualifications can you justify their need in objective terms? That is, why do you want those specific qualifications?

(Q) Have you made it clear you will consider equivalent or similar level alternative qualifications?

Ⓠ Is it clear that degrees or diplomas obtained abroad are acceptable, if they are of an equivalent standard to UK qualifications?

Ⓠ If you have specified that you want a graduate, have you made it clear that you are interested in the qualification and not the age of the applicant? The term 'graduate' can be interpreted as code for someone in their early twenties but graduates can be almost any age.

Ⓠ Is the relative importance placed on each criterion, and whether it is essential or desirable, made clear?

Ⓠ As far as possible, are all the criteria capable of being tested objectively? This means avoiding vague or subjective qualities. Attributes such as 'leadership', which are widely used in the selection process, need to be precisely and objectively defined in terms of the measurable skills and qualities that contribute to it; for example, fairness, knowledge, diplomacy, imagination and decisiveness.

Ⓠ Have you avoided any terms that reflect personal preferences rather than justifiable requirements?

Ⓠ Have you reviewed any existing candidate specifications before using them again, to make sure the requirements and criteria applied are still relevant?

brilliant tip

One of the best ways to ensure your candidate specification is not discriminatory is to have it checked and signed off by the person responsible for equal opportunities in the organisation, or in smaller companies this might be the director or owner.

Sourcing candidates

It makes sound business sense to attract a wide field of applicants – if you rely on the friends or family of current staff you will miss the opportunity to tap into the diverse skills of your local community and the wider market. It could also be seen as potentially discriminatory if you recruit solely, or in the first instance, on the basis of recommendations by existing staff, particularly when the workforce is wholly or predominantly from one racial group.

Advertising

It is unlawful to publish or order to be published an advertisement that indicates or might reasonably be understood as indicating an intention to discriminate unlawfully on any of the grounds outlined above.

If you are responsible for writing a recruitment advertisement, whether for a website, the press, a notice board, on your shop door or anywhere else, ask yourself the questions below and then rectify the ad accordingly:

Ⓠ Is your advertisement worded in such a way that it will encourage applicants from both sexes, all ages, all races, etc.?

Ⓠ Is it jargon-free and written in a way that everyone will understand?

Ⓠ Are you placing the advertisement in publications likely to reach all groups?

Ⓠ Are you advertising widely, fairly and openly so as to attract applicants from all backgrounds, age, race, etc.?

 **example**

An advertisement placed only in a magazine aimed at young people may indirectly discriminate against older people because they are less likely to subscribe to the magazine and therefore less likely to find out about the vacancy and apply.

Q Have you reviewed all advertising material and accompanying literature relating to employment to ensure that it avoids discrimination, for example presenting men and women in stereotyped roles? As well as considering the language you use in adverts, think also about the hidden messages that may be present in any promotional literature that you have, particularly the pictures.

Q Has your Human Resources or Personnel Department approved the advert? They are the experts.

Q If you do not have in-house expertise have you got someone else to read it objectively to see if they can see any form of discrimination? (Make sure they are aware of what discrimination covers.) Publications can also be held liable for discriminating in what they publish, so ask for their advice.

Q Have you included a reference to your organisation's equal opportunity policy, if you have one?

Q Have you written your job advert using the information in the job description and candidate specification?

Q Have you avoided using language that might imply that you would prefer someone of a certain age, such as 'mature', 'young' or 'energetic'?

Q If you were an ordinary member of the public reading this advertisement, would you think it was discriminatory in any way?

Recruitment consultancies

You need to ensure that you are not briefing a recruitment consultancy in any way that may be discriminatory. If you have put together a job and candidate definition that you have ensured is not discriminatory, then use this to brief the agency. They are also bound by law to work in a totally non-discriminatory way and should refuse to accept instructions from you that counter this.

You should not make comments, spoken or written, that could be discriminating and you should avoid giving preferences where these are discriminatory even if you feel you have a valid reason for stating them.

brilliant example

The team you are recruiting for is predominantly women and you mention to your recruitment consultant that you would prefer to restore the balance by recruiting a man. As there is no justifiable reason for this, it is discriminatory.

Equally if the members of your team are all under 25 you may state that you would prefer someone of the same age so that they fit in better. Again, there is no justifiable reason for this and so it is discriminatory.

Your recruitment process

The arrangements made for deciding who should be offered a job, your recruitment process, should be fair to all applicants and should not discriminate in any way either directly or indirectly.

your recruitment process should be fair to all applicants and should not discriminate directly or indirectly

Ask yourself, does my recruitment procedure include the following?

- Are the applicants all being given the same information?
- Are they all going through the same process?
- Are the other people involved in the selection process aware of what constitutes discrimination and what our policies are regarding this?
- Is each individual being assessed according to his or her personal capability to carry out the job?

First and subsequent interviews

Up until the interview stage you can check and re-check what you are doing to ensure that it is not discriminatory. When conducting an interview you are on the spot, and if you ask a question or make an inappropriate remark it cannot be removed or re-worded.

As we saw in Chapter 5, by planning you can make sure that you get all the information you need to make an assessment of the candidate. Because planning helps you to focus on gathering the information it will also help to ensure you do not inadvertently ask or use discriminatory wording.

You can avoid some of the pitfalls by recognising areas that could be a potential problem.

---

brilliant example

You are recruiting a buyer who will have to do extensive and prolonged travel to the Far East so it is necessary to ensure the candidates are aware of this and that they can meet this requirement. Explain the situation and discuss it objectively. Ask if the candidate has any difficulties meeting this requirement. Do not ask questions based on assumptions about marital status, children and domestic obligations such as 'Will you be able to arrange for someone to look after your children while you are away?' Ask all the candidates the same question and not just those you know or think have other commitments such as children.

Points to follow are:

- Plan your interview to ensure that your questions relate to the requirements of the job.
- Try to have more than one person involved in the interviews to ensure that any personal preferences and prejudices are not allowed to affect the decision on whom to hire.

- Make sure that all interviewers are aware of what can constitute discrimination and how to avoid it.

- Avoid asking questions that can be discriminatory such as those related to age, for example, 'How would you feel about managing older / younger people?'

- Avoid throw-away comments such as 'You're a bit young for a post of this responsibility', or 'Don't you think someone like you should be looking for something with more responsibility?'

- Avoid any questions that could be discriminatory such as those about marriage plans or family intentions, as these could discriminate against women.

- Make your decisions about who to call back for the next interview or who to offer to, based on the applicants' skills and competence.

- Check decisions for any bias. Before moving on to the next stage of the recruitment process, check that no bias, deliberate or unintentional, has influenced decisions. Ideally this check should be carried out by someone who has not been involved in the short-listing.

- Record your decisions and retain these records, ideally for 12 months from the date of the interviews.

Tests and practical tasks

If selection tests are used, they should be specifically related to job and / or career requirements and should measure an individual's actual or inherent ability to do or train for the work or career.

Tests should be reviewed regularly to ensure that they remain relevant and free from any unjustifiable bias, either in content or in scoring mechanism.

Practical tasks should also be directly related to the job and be used to identify specific abilities such as presentation abilities, telephone skills, written skills, etc., only if they are necessary to complete the job satisfactorily.

The offer

The job offer is also covered by discrimination legislation and it is illegal to discriminate in any way in the terms of employment including the benefits, facilities or services offered. The most obvious example of this will be offering different levels of pay to men and women or offering a company car to one but not the other. It could include, for example, part-time work, domestic leave, company cars and benefits for dependants and should be available to both male and female employees in the same or similar role.

If you employ part-time workers where they do not enjoy pro-rata pay or benefits with full-time workers, the arrangements should be reviewed to ensure that they are justified without regard to sex.

Review all terms of employment, benefits, facilities and services to ensure that there is no unlawful discrimination.

 **summary**

- Be aware of what discrimination is and make sure others involved are also aware.
- Try to involve more than one person at each stage of the selection process.
- Make sure that your job and candidate specification include only tasks, duties and requirements necessary for the job.
- Treat all candidates equally and put them through the same process.
- Ask yourself at every stage if what you are doing, writing or saying could be adversely affecting certain groups and therefore discriminatory.
- Plan your interview so that you are asking relevant questions.
- Make sure that your salary and benefits package is the same for men and women.

Index of questions

Questions to candidates about present and previous companies

Questions establishing level of seniority

Questions to establish how they are managed

Questions about specific duties and responsibilities

Questions regarding 'gaps' and anomalies on CVs

Questions on dismissal

Questions on education

Questions on work placements

Questions on hobbies and interests

Questions on college leavers' reasons for applying to you

Questions relating to organisational ability

Questions to assess communication skills

Questions on financial skills

Questions on sales skills and ability

Questions on technical ability

Questions on their ability to influence others

Questions on leadership skills

Questions on team work

Questions on planning skills

Questions to assess whether they are lively, studious, outgoing

Questions to assess their tenacity to get things done

Questions to establish if they have an eye for detail

Questions to assess analytical ability

Questions to assess confidentiality

Questions to establish honesty

Questions on external relationships

Questions on overcoming difficult working relationships

Questions on career progression

Questions about success

Questions on their reasons for applying for your vacancy

Questions about their knowledge of your company and market sector

Questions on specialist roles

Questions on time management

Questions on influencing and relationships

Questions on finance

Questions on strategy planning

Questions about working across multi functions

Questions on market knowledge

Questions about travel and re-location

Questions about salary and notice period

the brilliant series

Fast and engaging, the *Brilliant* series works hard to make sure you stand out from the crowd. Each *Brilliant* book has been carefully crafted to ensure everything you read is practical and applicable – to help you make a difference now.

9780273722328

9780273730675

9780273714637

9780273720591

9780273717355

9780273719144

9780273721826

9780273720799

9780273712350

9780273714842

9780273726463

9780273725114

9780273721239

- Fast Learning – making the complex simple in the quickest time possible

- Outcome Focused – tells you only what you need to know and do to make a difference

- Practical – rather than theoretical. It's about putting the skills into practice

Whatever your level, we'll get you to the next one.
It's all about you. Get ready to shine!

PEARSON
Prentice Hall
BUSINESS